RUSHING
TO
RMAGEDDON

E SHOCKING TRUTH ABOUT

ANADA, MISSILE DEFENCE,

AND STAR WARS

MEL HURTIG

M&S

Copyright © 2004 by Mel Hurtig

All rights reserved. The use of any part of this publication reproduced, transmitted in any form or by any means, electronic, mechanical, photoco recording, or otherwise, or stored in a retrieval system, without the prior consent of the publisher – or, in case of photocopying or other reprograph copying, a licence from the Canadian Copyright Licensing Agency – is an infringement of the copyright law.

National Library of Canada Cataloguing in Publication

Hurtig, Mel
    Rushing to Armageddon : the shocking truth about Canada, Missile D and Star Wars / Mel Hurtig.

ISBN 0-7710-4162-4

    1. Strategic Defense Initiative. 2. Space weapons. 3. United States –
Military policy. 4. Canada – Military policy. I. Title.

UG745.C3H87 2004   358'.8'0973   C2004-902916-9

We acknowledge the financial support of the Government of Canada throu Book Publishing Industry Development Program and that of the Governme Ontario through the Ontario Media Development Corporation's Ontario B Initiative. We further acknowledge the support of the Canada Council for tl Arts and the Ontario Arts Council for our publishing program.

Typeset in Minion by M&S, Toronto
Printed and bound in Canada

This book is printed on acid-free paper that is 100% recycled,
ancient-forest friendly (100% post-consumer recycled).

McClelland & Stewart Ltd.
The Canadian Publishers
481 University Avenue
Toronto, Ontario
M5G 2E9
www.mcclelland.com

  2 3 4 5   08 07 06 05 04

For
Mary-Wynne Ashford, Rosalie Bertell,
Stephen Lewis, John Polanyi,
Ernie Regehr, Douglas Roche

and the many other wonderful Canadians who have worked so long
and so hard in the cause of peace and disarmament.

AUGUSTANA LIBRARY
UNIVERSITY OF ALBERTA

CONTENTS

ACKNOWLEDGEMENTS

I would very much like to thank my wife, Kay Hurtig, and all of the following who helped me with this book including Julie Maloney, Linda Grisley, Senator Douglas Roche, Ernie Regehr, Ambassador Christopher Westdal, my editors Jonathan Webb and Elizabeth Kribs, my former publisher Doug Gibson, Willem Hubben, Frank Cunningham, Robert S. Rodvik, Leslie Hurtig, Douglas Mattern, Steven Staples, John M. Clearwater, David Estrin, and the following authors, journalists, and commentators whose work I have quoted: David Pugliese, Paul Krugman, Linda McQuaig, Bruce Blair, James Hecht, John Steinbruner, Jim Stoffels, John Godfrey, John Polanyi, John Isaacs, Alexander Zaitchik, Fred Kaplan, Jeffrey Simpson, Tom Walkom, Lloyd Axworthy, Tariq Rauf, Terrence Paupp, Paul Hellyer, Geov Parrish, Glen Milner, Michael Costello, Melvin Goodman, Leo Satori, Lester R. Brown, Richard Gwyn, Noam Chomsky, David Francis, Andrew Cohen, Lisbeth Gronlund, Alex Shepherd, Charles Caccia, Seymour Hersh, John le Carré, Arthur Terry, Loring Wirbel, Joseph Fitchell, John Laughland, Stephen Lewis, Gregory Kerr, John Robert Colombo, Jody Williams, Dr. Paul Hamel, and Dr. John Valleau.

Brief Biographies of
Some of the Cited Authorities

Mary Wynne-Ashford, M.D., Ph.D., palliative care physician, two Governor-General medals, Gandhi Award from Simon Fraser University, Honourary Citizen of Victoria. Most notably peace activist who was co-president of the International Physicians for the Prevention of Nuclear Weapons, the organization that won the Nobel Peace Prize in 1985. Dr. Ashford teaches Global Education and Violence Prevention at the University of Victoria.

Lloyd Axworthy, former Manitoba MLA, former Liberal member of Parliament (1979–2000), numerous cabinet posts notably Minister of Foreign Affairs from 1996–2000, CEO Liu Centre for the Study of Global Issues at U.B.C. Now president of the University of Winnipeg.

Rosalie Bertell, B.A., M.A., Ph.D., D. Hum. Lit., LL.D, President International Institute of Concern for Public Health, numerous international awards and honours including Women of Distinction Award, World Federalist Canada Peace Award, author, editor, scholar, widely respected public health consultant and expert on nuclear dangers.

Bruce G. Blair, Ph.D., is president of the Center for Defense Information, formerly for thirteen years senior fellow in Foreign Policy Studies at the Brookings Institution. An expert on U.S. and Russian security policies and command-control systems. Frequently testifies before Congress. Taught security studies at Yale and Princeton. Author of numerous books and articles on security issues.

Niels Bohr, Danish Nobel laureate, a key figure in the Manhattan Project, one of the foremost scientists of modern physics, and a leading figure in the development of the quantum theory. Awarded Nobel Prize in Physics in 1922. Fled Nazi-occupied Denmark to U.S. in 1943, returning after World War II in 1945.

Lester R. Brown is the founder of the Washington, D.C.-based Earth Policy Institute. The *Washington Post* described him as "one of the world's most influential thinkers."

McGeorge Bundy was a high-profile special assistant for national security affairs to U.S. president John F. Kennedy, and then president Lyndon Johnson. In both positions he played a major role in the evolution of U.S. foreign policy.

Noam Chomsky, educator, linguist, political commentator, popular and prolific best-selling author. Professor of linguistics and philosophy at MIT. "Arguably the most important intellectual alive" – *New York Times*.

Mohamed ElBaradei, Director General of the United Nations International Atomic Energy Agency (IAEA), headquartered in Vienna since 1997. Former Egyptian diplomat. Doctor in international law from New York University. He monitors nuclear programs around the world, including the nuclear capacity of North Korea and Iran. Worked with weapons inspector Hans Blix in Iraq.

John Godfrey, M.P., D.Phil., D. Litt.S, Liberal Member of Parliament from Toronto since 1993. Was appointed Parliamentary Secretary to the Prime Minister, responsible for cities, in December 2003. Formerly President and Vice-Chancellor University of King's College, Editor the *Financial Post* 1987–1991.

Melvin Goodman is senior fellow at the Center for International Policy in Washington, D.C., and co-author with Craig Eisendrath of the 2004 book *Bush League Diplomacy: How the Neoconservatives Are Putting the World at Risk* (Prometheus Books).

Dr. Lisbeth Gronlund is a Senior Scientist and Co-director of the Global Security Program at the Union of Concerned Scientists in Cambridge, Massachusetts, and a Research Scientist in the Massachusetts Institute of Technology (MIT) Security Studies Program. She holds a Ph.D. in physics from Cornell University and is a Fellow of the American Physical Society. Her recent research has focused on technical issues related to ballistic missile defences, international fissile material controls, and new nuclear weapons proposed by the Bush administration. She has published widely in scientific and policy journals, given numerous talks about nuclear weapons and missile defence policy issues to both lay and expert audiences, and testified to Congress.

James L. Hecht has a Ph.D. in chemical engineering from Yale and in 1985 became Adjunct Professor in political science at the University of Delaware. Later he moved to Denver and became a senior fellow at the Center for Public Policy and Contemporary Issues at the University of Denver. He has published extensively on U.S.-Russian relations, military budgets, and civil rights.

Stephen Lewis, former Ontario MPP and provincial NDP leader. Canadian Ambassador to United Nations 1984–88. Special Advisor to UN Secretary-General 1986–91, UNICEF, including Deputy Executive Director 1995–99; appointed by UN as Special Envoy on AIDS in Africa, 2001. Member International Panel of Eminent Persons.

Douglas Mattern is President of the Association of World Citizens, a San Francisco-based international peace organization with branches in over thirty countries.

Linda McQuaig, author and journalist. McQuaig's column appears every Sunday in the *Toronto Star* and frequently in the *Edmonton Journal*. She is the widely read author of several best-selling Canadian books.

Terrence Edward Paupp is a Nuclear Age Peace Foundation Policy Analyst; National Chancellor of the United States for the International Association of Educators for World Peace, and is professor of politics and international law, National University, San Diego, CA. Author of *Achieving Inclusionary Governance* (Transnational Publishers, 2000).

John Polanyi, P.C., C.C., Ph.D., D.Sc., LL.D, F.R.S., widely respected academic and prolific writer and researcher. Nobel Prize for Chemistry 1986, dozens of international awards and honours. Founding member Canadian Pugwash Committee, consultant, lecturer, and long-time activist for peace and disarmament. University professor at University of Toronto.

Tariq Rauf is the Head, Verification and Security Policy Coordination, International Atomic Energy Agency (IAEA), Vienna. Responsible for policy co-ordination on nuclear non-proliferation, safeguards, disarmament, security, and related verification and implementation matters. Former Director of International Organizations and Nonproliferation Program at Monterey Institute of International Studies. Widely educated and travelled consultant and lecturer, with numerous publications. A Canadian with doctoral studies and research at the University of Toronto.

Ernie Regehr is the indefatigable Executive Director of Project Ploughshares, and a long-time campaigner for peace and disarmament. Project Ploughshares was formed to implement the Canadian churches' imperative to pursue peace and justice, to help develop approaches that build peace and prevent war, and to promote the peaceful resolution of political conflict. Recently awarded Order of Canada.

Douglas Roche, O.C., served as Member of Parliament from 1972 to 1984, and was appointed to the Senate in 1998. He was Canada's Ambassador for Disarmament from 1984 to 1989, and was elected Chairman of the UN Disarmament Committee in 1988. He is currently Chairman of the Middle Powers Initiative. He has received a long list of international awards, medals, and other honours for his untiring work on behalf of peace and disarmament. He is the author of seventeen books, the latest, *The Human Right to Peace* (Novalis, 2003).

Leo Satori is emeritus professor of physics at the University of Nebraska-Lincoln. From 1978 until 1981 he served at the U.S. Arms Control and Disarmament Agency, and took part in the Salt II negotiations.

Jim Stoffels is co-founder and chairman of World Citizens for Peace in Richland, Washington – the only peace and nuclear disarmament organization at the Hanford Nuclear Site, where plutonium was pro-duced for the Nagasaki atomic bomb and most of the U.S. nuclear arsenal. He is a retired research physicist from the U.S. Department of Energy's National Laboratory at Hanford.

Christopher Westdal, diplomat, formerly Canadian Ambassador to the United Nations in Geneva and Ambassador for Disarmament. Now Canada's Ambassador to Russia. Formerly High Commissioner to Bangladesh, Ambassador to Burma, South Africa, and Ukraine.

Loring Wirbel has been involved in peace and disarmament work for twenty-five years. He is now editorial director for communications at CMP Media headquartered in London and New York, and has extensive intelligence, civil liberties, and technology experience.

ACRONYMS AND ABBREVIATIONS

ABM	Anti-ballistic missile
BMD	Ballistic missile defence
CCCE	Canadian Council of Chief Executives (formerly the Business Council on National Issues)
CIA	Central Intelligence Agency
CIP	Center for International Policy
CTBT	Comprehensive Test-Ban Treaty
DFAIT	Department of Foreign Affairs and International Trade
IAEA	International Atomic Energy Agency
ICBM	Intercontinental ballistic missile
MAD	Mutual assured destruction
MDA	Missile Defense Agency
MIRV	Multiple independently-targeted re-entry vehicle
NMD	The American National Missile Defense program of ballistic missile defence
NORAD	North American Aerospace Defence Command
NPT	Non-Proliferation Treaty
SDI	Ronald Reagan's Strategic Defense Initiative
WMD	Weapons of mass destruction
WTO	World Trade Organization

PREFACE

———————■———————

Never was the danger as great as today.
An atomic war draws nearer . . .
　　　　　　　　　　　– Mohamed ElBaradei, January 2004

From Reuters, February 2, 2004:

President George W. Bush is planning to put the first weapons in space despite broad international opposition, budget papers sent to Congress on Monday showed.

China, an emerging space power, has voiced strong objections to such "weaponization" of space as have Russia and some European allies.

The fiscal 2005 budget is the first to set aside funds to start developing the kind of weapons President Ronald Reagan had in mind when he called for a space-based Strategic Defense Initiative. Critics decried Reagan's vision as "Star Wars."

From *Hansard*, February 19, 2004, Hon. Bill Graham (Minister of Foreign Affairs, Lib.):

We are entering into negotiations and discussions with the United States . . . We are not in any way engaged in, nor will we permit ourselves to be engaged in, anything to do with the weaponization of space. It is a defence system. There is no reason to suggest that this will result in the weaponization of space. [*]

This book is about how Paul Martin and his Liberal government have misled Canadians about one of the most vitally important decisions in the 137-year history of our country, and how Stephen Harper and the Conservatives want Canada to quickly and enthusiastically join the American Star Wars and other military plans. (For more on Harper and the Conservatives, see the chapter "Moving by Stealth to Co-operate in Our Own Ghastly Annihilation.")

In what follows, the charge that the Martin government has not been candid with Canadians is a strong one. But this opinion is based on abundant research and substantial documentation of discounted or ignored clear evidence that the United States intends to put weapons into space, that American missile "defence" plans are leading to a dangerous new arms race and nuclear proliferation, that rather than helping to protect Canada, the U.S. plans will endanger Canadians. And, in the greatest irony, all this about a missile defence program that does not, and cannot, work.

In recent months many Canadians have become increasingly concerned about the terrible dangers of nuclear proliferation, military escalation, and global destabilization, most of it due to American plans to weaponize and dominate space, and to completely "deny others the use of space."

---

[*] As this book was going to the printer Paul Martin moved Bill Graham from the Foreign Affairs portfolio to Defence, replacing the former defence minister David Pratt who was defeated in the June federal election. Taking Graham's place in Foreign Affairs is Pierre Pettigrew, widely regarded as unreservedly pro-American. Pettigrew has forcefully called for closer and deeper economic and defence ties with the U.S. When the Cancún trade talks collapsed due to widespread worldwide opposition, Pettigrew announced "In Cancún, I really felt like I have never loved the Americans so much."

We are far from being alone in our fears of potential cataclysmic disaster. In January 2004, Mohamed ElBaradei, head of the United Nations International Atomic Energy Agency, said in an interview with *Der Spiegel* magazine that the threat of nuclear war is greater today than it ever has been.

> Never was the danger as great as today. An atomic war draws nearer if we do not start thinking about a new international control system.
>
> I worry that in our collective memories, the horrors of Hiroshima and Nagasaki are beginning to fade.

In April of 2003, the mayor of Hiroshima, Tadatoshi Akiba, predicted that

> We stand on the brink of hyper-proliferation and perhaps the third actual use of nuclear weapons, and the unspeakable violence and misery that will follow.
>
> We are now forced to conclude that the United States, the prime mover in all things nuclear, relentlessly and blatantly intends to maintain, develop, and even use these heinous, illegal weapons.

Later in this book you will find a quote from a Canadian Department of National Defence briefing for the minister: "BMD [ballistic missile defence] is perhaps one of the most important security questions the government will have to consider."

In March of this year, in an afterword to a new book published by the University of Calgary Press, I wrote that the very future of an independent Canada will be jeopardized if we make the fatal mistake of joining the American Star Wars plans.* I hope *Rushing to Armageddon* will contribute in a meaningful way to what will inevitably be one of the

---

* The article titled "Foreign and Defence Policy Independence: Will This Be Our Very Last Chance?" appears in *Canada and the New American Empire*, edited by George Melnyk.

most contentious issues in Canada since the free-trade debates of the mid- to late-1980s.

It is not without good reasons that this book is dedicated to, among others, Douglas Roche and Ernie Regehr, two truly great Canadians, who have worked unceasingly for much of their lives for peace and disarmament and for the abolition of nuclear weapons.

I have written this book because I fear that aggressive American militarism and the undeniable U.S. plans for the weaponization of space are rapidly leading the world towards nuclear carnage. Many who read the book will already know why I am now so apprehensive and will share that apprehension, but most will likely be unfamiliar with much of what they will encounter on the pages that follow.

Sadly, most will also be unfamiliar with the true dimensions of the devastation caused by nuclear weapons. Many have forgotten the horrendous events of August 1945, while many others have not had the catastrophic details imprinted on their minds. It is for this reason that I begin with an excerpt from Douglas Roche's excellent book *The Ultimate Evil*,[*] followed by some words from a recent important document by Ernie Regehr.

When you read what follows do understand that the thousands of nuclear weapons now in silos, in bombers, on mobile rail cars, and on ships and submarines, range from thirty to well over three hundred times the destructive power of the Hiroshima and Nagasaki bombs.

And do understand, as you will see in the pages that follow, that the defeat of George W. Bush in the November presidential election will very likely not bring the salvation that most Canadians hope for and anticipate.

Ultimately, the decision about Canada's participation in the American missile defence plans may not have been made in the House of Commons, but in Paul Martin's office. Martin has never been committed to a parliamentary vote on the issue, and the results of the June 28 federal election may not change this. Even if Jack Layton and the NDP

---

[*] James Lorimer, 1997.

were successful in demanding a Commons vote, the combined Liberal and Conservative vote would likely overwhelm the votes of the combined NDP, Bloc, and those Liberals who oppose Canada's involvement.

Meanwhile, the Prime Minister has been under heavy and sustained pressure. Two days after the election, U.S. Ambassador Paul Cellucci warned Canadians that "the clock is definitely ticking" in Washington. We should let it tick. Paul Martin repeatedly promised that "Canadians are entitled to be consulted" and that no final decision would be made before a thorough, informed national debate. To date, as we shall see in what follows, the government has failed miserably to provide Canadians with enough reliable information to allow such a debate to take place.

AN ASSAULT ON HUMANITY

By Douglas Roche

After a while, countless men, women and children began to gather for a drink of water at the banks of nearby Urakami River, their hair and clothing scorched and their burnt skin hanging off in sheets like rags. Begging for help, they died one after another in the water or in heaps on the banks. Then radiation began to take its toll, killing people like a scourge of death expanding in concentric circles from the hypocenter. Four months after the atomic bombing, 74,000 people were dead and 75,000 had suffered injuries, that is, two-thirds of the city population had fallen victim to this calamity that came upon Nagasaki like a preview of the Apocalypse.

— Mayor Icco Itoh, Nagasaki, 1997

When I visited Mayor Takashi Hiraoka of Hiroshima and Mayor Icco Itoh of Nagasaki during a trip to Japan in the spring of 1997, I asked each of them for a message to the Canadian Parliamentary Committee on Foreign Affairs and International Trade, which was then beginning a review of Canada's policies on nuclear weapons. Mayor Hiraoka wrote the Committee: "We, the citizens of Hiroshima, who have suffered a nuclear bombing, deeply believe that the development and possession of nuclear weapons is a crime against humanity, and that nuclear weapons and humankind cannot coexist." Mayor Itoh replied: "Based on our experience, the people of Nagasaki have been appealing to the world that nuclear weapons are lethal, that they could annihilate the human race, and that genuine world peace cannot be attained as long as nuclear weapons exist on this planet."

The logic of the case for the elimination of nuclear weapons is overpowering, but logic by itself moves neither governments nor the public. In fact, my own views are more strongly rooted in the human dimensions of the Hiroshima and Nagasaki tragedies than they are in logic. I was sixteen when the first atomic bombs were dropped on Hiroshima and Nagasaki in early August 1945. It was only years later, on my first visit to Japan in the mid-1970s, that the horror and scale of the destruction made a lasting impression on me. As the years go by, memories of World War II dim and I notice that my students deal with the destructive capacity of nuclear weapons in an even more superficial and abstract way.

If the modern movement to abolish nuclear weapons is to make an imprint on the general public, the unimaginable horror of nuclear weapons must be faced. Mayors Hiraoka and Itoh have done a service to this movement by bringing the full story of nuclear devastation to the World Court. In 1994, the World Court was asked to decide on the legality of nuclear weapons. The Mayors' testimonies were given as evidence in the case. Here are the stories they told.[*]

At 8:15 on the fateful morning of August 6, 1945, as World War II was drawing to a close in the Pacific, the American atomic bomb exploded 580 meters above the heart of Hiroshima. It contained a small amount of uranium-235 and produced the energy equivalent of 15,000 tons (15 kilotons) of TNT. An intense flash of light flooded the city center. With the roar that followed, enormous pillars of flame burst toward the skies, as most buildings crumbled and many

---

[*] Quoted in Douglas Roche, *The Ultimate Evil* (James Lorimer, 1997).

people died or were injured. Old and young, male and female, soldier and civilian – the killing was utterly indiscriminate. The entire city was exposed to the compound and devastating effects of thermal rays, shock-wave blast, and radiation.

The Hiroshima bomb generated intense heat that shot out from a fireball about 280 meters wide. The thermal rays emanating from it instantly charred any human being outdoors near the hypocenter (the surface point directly below the explosion). As far as two kilometers from the hypocenter people's clothing burst into flames. Fires ignited simultaneously across the city, reducing it to char and ashes.

After the initial shock wave, an extremely powerful wind of nearly 1,000 miles per hour tore through the city. People were lifted and carried through the air by this blast. All wooden buildings within a radius of about two kilometers collapsed: many well beyond that distance were badly damaged. The blast and thermal rays combined to totally burn or collapse 70 per cent of the 76,327 dwellings in Hiroshima at the time.

There was also radiation damage. Immediately after the explosion, the area was bathed in high levels of initial radiation – gamma rays and neutrons. Within a radius of about one kilometer of the hypocenter, nearly everyone who suffered full body exposure to radiation died. Those who initially managed to survive soon succumbed to the radiation's after-effects. Many not directly exposed to the bomb approached the hypocenter to offer help and sickened or died due to residual radiation. Even today, thousands of people struggle daily with the curse of radiation sickness.

On August 6, there were approximately 350,000 people in Hiroshima. Some 140,000 of them were dead by the end of December 1945. Entire families were wiped out, and the local community was in disarray. Records were lost to fire, and so even today we have no truly accurate figures. Among the dead were Koreans, Chinese, students from throughout Asia, and even a few American prisoners of war.

Hospitals were in ruins, medical staff were dead or injured, and there were no medicines or equipment. Despite their own burns and injuries survivors worked frantically to help others, but after a few days or weeks, fever, diarrhea, hemorrhaging, and extreme fatigue claimed many more lives. This was the pattern of the acute symptoms of A-bomb disease. Along with burns and external injuries, initial radiation brought disease and other maladies. Those exposed near the hypocenter suffered widespread destruction of cells and loss of blood, resulting in tissue and organ damage. Immune systems were weakened and symptoms like hair loss were conspicuous.

These acute effects subsided after about four months, but five to six years after the bombing a dramatic increase in leukemia and other later effects were recorded. Keloids (excessive growth of scar tissue over healed burns), cataracts, and various cancers added to the death toll. Those exposed in their mothers' wombs were often born with microcephalia, a syndrome involving mental retardation and incomplete growth.

Sadako Sasaki was exposed to the bomb at the age of two. She appeared to grow up strong and healthy, but ten years later, in 1955, she was suddenly diagnosed with leukemia and hospitalized. Cranes are a symbol of longevity in Japan and Sadako believed she would be healed if she folded 1,000 paper cranes, so every day, lying in bed using the paper her medicine came in, she folded cranes. Despite her hopes and efforts, she died after eight months of fighting.

Mayor Itoh's testimony to the World Court told of how, three days after the Hiroshima attack, an American bomber abandoned its primary target of Kokura because of poor visibility and flew to its secondary target, Nagasaki. That city was also covered by clouds, but the plane was running short of fuel so when the bombardier caught a glimpse of the city through a crack in the clouds, he hastily released the second atomic bomb.

The Urakami district of Nagasaki was home to a large Christian population that had kept the light of faith alive during a long period of persecution from the seventeenth through the nineteenth centuries. The bomb laid the neighbourhood to waste and instantly killed 8,500 of the 12,000 Christians living there. It was later discovered that the original target for the bombing had not been the Urakami district, which lies in the northern part of Nagasaki, but rather the very centre of the city. If the bomb had exploded over the densely populated city centre, Nagasaki likely would have been obliterated.

The Mayor of Nagasaki at the time recorded the effect of the explosion:

> The explosion of the atomic bomb generated an enormous fireball, 200 metres in radius, almost as though a small sun had appeared in the sky. The next instant, a ferocious blast and wave of heat assailed the ground with a thunderous roar. The surface temperature of the fireball was above 7,000°C, and the heat rays that reached the ground were over 3,000°C. The explosion instantly killed or injured people within a two-kilometre radius of the hypocenter, leaving innumerable corpses charred like clumps of charcoal and scattered in the ruins near the hypocenter. In some cases not even a trace of the person's remains could be found. A wind of over 680 miles per hour slapped down trees and demolished most buildings. Even iron-reinforced concrete structures were so badly damaged that they seemed to have been smashed by a giant hammer. The fierce flash of heat meanwhile melted glass and left metal objects contorted like strands of taffy, and the subsequent fires burned the ruins of the city to ashes. Nagasaki became a city of death where not even the sounds of insects could be heard.
>
> After a while, countless men, women and children began to gather for a drink of water at the banks of nearby Urakami River, their hair and clothing scorched and their burnt skin hanging off in sheets like rags. Begging for help, they died one after another in the water or in heaps on the banks. Then radiation began to take its toll, killing people like a scourge of death expanding in concentric circles from the hypocenter. Four months after the atomic bombing, 74,000

people were dead and 75,000 had suffered injuries, that is, two-thirds of the city population had fallen victim to this calamity that came upon Nagasaki like a preview of the Apocalypse.

The air-raid shelter in Sakamoto-machi was filled with the dead and injured. The area near the shelter was strewn with corpses, some scorched black and others half-naked with puffed-up faces and skin hanging off like rags. It filled me with sorrow to see, among these, the corpses of a mother clinging to her newborn baby and her three other children lying dead nearby. I could do nothing for the people screaming for help from under the ruins of houses or the people crawling along the ground dragging their burnt skin and begging for water. These screams of agony in the throes of death echoed in the ruins all night. When my father found a pot in the ruins and used it to draw from a stream, the injured drank it greedily but then lay down and died on the ground. The following morning the screams had subsided, leaving only a world of death like a hell on Earth.

The most fundamental difference between nuclear and conventional weapons is that the former release radioactive rays at the time of explosion. Everyone exposed to large doses of radiation generated during the first minute after the Nagasaki explosion died within two weeks. Not only people directly exposed, but also those who came into the area of the hypocentre after the bombing and those exposed to fallout carried by the wind, suffered radiation-induced injuries. A high incidence of disease was observed among survivors exposed to large doses of radiation. Leukemia, malignant tumours, and other maladies appeared after long periods of latency. The descendants of survivors will have to be monitored by several generations to clarify the genetic impact, and so generations to come will be forced to live in anxiety.

Nagasaki Mayor Itoh concluded his description of the atomic bomb's effects on his city by telling the World Court:

With their colossal power and capacity for slaughter and destruction, nuclear weapons make no distinction between combatants and non-combatants or between military installations and civilian communities; moreover, the radiation released by these weapons cannot be confined to specific military targets. It can only be said, therefore, that nuclear weapons are inhuman tools for mass slaughter and destruction.

History's Worst Possible Nightmare

------■------

*I want to describe to you what's at stake – which is, not to put too
fine a point on it, everything.*
                            – Ambassador Christopher Westdal, March 2000

Douglas Mattern, renowned peace activist from San Francisco, writes:

Today, both Russia and the U.S. have thousands of nuclear warheads
on a hair-trigger alert, ready to launch within a few minutes' notice.
The Center for Defense Information (CDI) in Washington, D.C.,
reports "if launched today, within minutes the two sides would be
firing at each other up to 4,000 high-yield nuclear warheads – the
explosive equivalent of nearly 100,000 Hiroshima bombs."

Consider this in the context of McGeorge Bundy's words in 1969:

In the real world, even one hydrogen bomb dropped on one city
would be a catastrophic blunder; ten bombs on ten cities would be
a disaster beyond history.*

---

* *Foreign Affairs*, vol. 48, no. 1, October 1969.

And, thousands of bombs? Bombs launched by intercontinental ballistic missiles from land and from sea, from cruise missiles and bombers, bombs detonated in containers in the holds of cargo ships or bombs placed on the upper floors of high office towers?

In a *Los Angeles Times* April 26, 2004 article titled "Still on Catastrophe's Edge," Robert McNamara and Helen Caldicott wrote:

> According to a report on nuclear war planning by the National Resources Defense Council, Russia aims most of its 8,200 nuclear warheads at the U.S., and the U.S. maintains 7,000 offensive strategic warheads in its arsenal.

Mattern continues:

> Utter madness! And yet in response to President Bush's intention to build the anti-missile system, the Russians sent a message by successfully test firing their Stiletto ICBM that can carry six warheads, each with 50 to 100 times the power of the Hiroshima bomb. The older ICBMs can carry 10-12 independently targeted nuclear warheads.

Meanwhile, U.S. Trident submarines which "provide the nation's most survivable and enduring nuclear strike capability" (there were eighteen of these in 2001) carry two dozen missiles that can launch almost two hundred nuclear warheads eight times the power of the Hiroshima bomb to two hundred separate targets. In Mattern's words, "Just one of these submarines is history's worst possible nightmare." And then this from a February 12, 2004 letter from Christopher Westdal:

> Hiroshima's "Little Boy" and Nagasaki's "Fat Man" averaged 15,000 tonnes TNT equivalent.
> What about the ratio between the Hiroshima bomb, a fissioning of uranium (the least stable natural element) and a thermonuclear bomb, a fusion of hydrogen (nature's most stable element): not 2 or 3, not tens or hundreds, but *thousands*.

It troubles me that the most popular image of what a nuclear weapon does to a city is dead wrong by whole orders of magnitude. Compared with megaton weapons, Little Boy and Fat Man were mere firecrackers.

And what would happen in a full-scale nuclear war where thousands of nuclear weapons were targeted at the developed world's cities? It's not difficult to calculate that most of the world's economy and its industrial capacity and most personal, corporate, and cultural assets of our civilization would be obliterated, along with much of the population in our cities around the world, while crop failure, disease, and radiation would decimate the rest of the globe. Nor is it difficult to foresee that the many millions of injured men, women, and children would suffer agonizing pain and death, without any medical help, and much of the world would be uninhabitable – a living hell of massive destruction and enveloping radiation – for decades.

Making Us and the World Less Secure

Deployments of the national missile defense system will likely tear up the fabric of arms control agreements which have improved global security for over thirty years.
– Center for International Policy, Washington, D.C., May 2001

Ernie Regehr has written a superb report, *Canada and Ballistic Missile Defence*, for the Liu Institute for Global Issues (December 2003).* In the report, Regehr writes

> Canadian policy has never focused on ballistic missile defence as a credible or even promising response to the threat of nuclear destruction via intercontinental ballistic missiles (ICBMs).
>
> Even so, Prime Minister Paul Martin said during his first press conference as leader of the Liberal Party that Canada needs to be at the table when Washington explores military measures . . .

Moreover, Regehr continues,

---

* To view the report go to www.ligi.ubc.ca

Mutually beneficial security cooperation between Canada and the United States neither depends on, nor is advanced by, the Canadian embrace of BMD.

Regehr goes on to explain that the American BMD system presently planned will protect against

only a tiny fraction (never more than about 1 per cent) of nuclear warheads capable of hitting targets in North America by means of strategic-range ballistic missiles.

Moreover the BMD system

will have no capacity (to protect) against short-range ballistic or cruise missiles that could be fired from ships a few hundred miles off North American coasts.

And,

the proposed system ignores the myriad of other ways in which weapons of mass destruction could be delivered to North American targets (for example, smuggled warheads in any one of the thousands of shipping containers that reach North America daily).

Most important of all,

the most realistic means of protecting Canadians from nuclear attacks are the same means the rest of the world must rely on – a focus on practical non-proliferation arms control and disarmament diplomacy.

It's vitally important to understand that

the BMD would be easily overwhelmed. BMD will drive emerging missile states to deploy many more missiles than they would have otherwise.

As for timing for a decision about Canada's role

there is nothing in the 2004–05 American deployment time frame that makes the present situation any more of a deadline or occasion for Canadian decision-making than any other period of BMD's tortured history.

And finally,

Canadian policy should recognize that strategic missile defence is counterproductive in that it so contributes to proliferation pressures.

I've hardly done justice to Ernie Regehr's detailed report, but the pages that follow elaborate on the key points raised by the many informed critics of the irresponsible and dangerous American plans.

Regehr refers to "BMD's tortured history." For at least forty years, Americans have been trying to develop a workable anti-ballistic missile system. Prior to the election of George W. Bush, the most concerted effort began during Ronald Reagan's first term as president.

The Strategic Defense Initiative, commonly referred to as "Star Wars," was announced by Reagan in a speech in March 1983. It was immediately attacked by critics as being hopelessly unrealistic. Numerous anti-ballistic missile technologies were researched and tested, including lasers, rocket-launched interceptors, space vehicles, and anti-decoy devices. Deployment was planned for no later than 2005, but numerous test failures, rapidly escalating costs, and a growing feeling that the program was unnecessary and a colossal waste of money resulted in its cancellation.

Through to the end of Bill Clinton's second term, the results were similar. But then, with the election of George W. Bush, a remarkable new dominating fixation surfaced. On September 5, 2001, columnist Maureen Dowd of the *New York Times* wrote: "Why can George W. Bush think of nothing but a missile shield? Our President is caught in the grip of an obsession worthy of literature."

Bear in mind that this was just six days before 9/11. And remember Dowd's description of Bush's mindset when you come to the chapter in this book on the *real* threat. Bush, by the way, in a major foreign policy speech in September 1999, promised that when he became president, his government would never get bogged down in "vague, aimless and endless [military] deployments." And, in relation to Iraq, in July 2003, U.S. Secretary of Defense Donald Rumsfeld said, "I don't do quagmires."*

---

* Maureen Dowd, *New York Times*, May 9, 2004.

"Secret," "Confidential," and "Canadian Eyes Only"

BMD is perhaps one of the most important security questions the government will have to consider.
— Department of National Defence briefing document

Late in January 2004, as a result of an Access to Information request, I received 306 pages of Department of National Defence briefing material from Ottawa. Two hundred and twenty-two pages were blank and marked "withheld." Almost all of the pages were labelled "secret" or "confidential" and "Canadian Eyes Only." Even the eighty-four pages containing text had missing words, missing sentences, and blanked-out paragraphs. Some of the material appears to have been prepared for cabinet, while much of it is in the form of briefing notes for defence minister John McCallum and his successor David Pratt.

In spite of all the material that was withheld, these documents still contain some fascinating and valuable insights.

First, it's quite clear that our Department of Defence had long ago made up its mind and strongly favours Canadian participation in the American BMD plans.

Second, in sharp contrast to what we've continually heard from our defence and foreign affairs ministers, U.S. "funding of space-based systems continues . . ."

Next, "none of the options Washington is currently pursuing for BMD would require direct Canadian participation (either in basing interceptors/radar or in using NORAD assets)."* The documents go on to explain that President Bush's plans are *far* more ambitious than those of any of his predecessors, with huge increases in annual spending (in 2004 more than double previous years) and with even larger increases planned in the future.

> Even under President Reagan's "Star Wars" effort, the most that Administration ever spent on missile defence was approximately $5 billion in adjusted dollars.

The briefing notes go on to explain that the 1972 ABM Treaty

> codified mutual vulnerability by prohibiting either side (Russia and the U.S.) from building nationwide missile defences . . . and placed limits prohibiting the number of interceptors which could be built, and also prohibited placing such systems on air or naval platforms, or in space.

However,

> the U.S. has withdrawn from the ABM Treaty, with a view to keeping all of its BMD options open.

It's important to understand that

---

* Air Force General Ralph Eberhart, NORAD commander, testified to the U.S. Senate on March 25, 2004, that the U.S. could do missile defence "without Canadian support."

Canada amended the NORAD agreement to specifically exclude Canada and NORAD from BMD activities – a policy that continues to this day.*

So far, the U.S.

has spent an estimated $100 billion since 1983 on missile defence research, and a similar amount in the 30 years before that.

What happened to the enthusiastic plans for Ronald Reagan's Star Wars defence system?

It was not implemented due to technological challenges, astronomical cost-estimates, and the end of the Cold War.

In December 2001,

believing that the ABM Treaty placed unreasonable limits on American options, Bush announced that the U.S. would exercise its right under the treaty and would withdraw effective the following June.

One obvious reason for the American decision is U.S. plans for military space-based weapons systems. Nevertheless, the Defence department documents play down any concern about the weaponizing of space, and somehow fail to mention the numerous official and public U.S. documents described in the pages that follow that clearly confirm American intentions to weaponize space, while affirming that

---

* This is not correct. In 1968, the Pearson government insisted that a new clause be added to the NORAD agreement that "will not involve in any way a Canadian commitment to participate in an active ballistic missile defence." However, this clause was dropped by the Trudeau government in 1981.

Many of the warning, detection, and communication elements of BMD have been, and continue to be, stationed in space.

Again, contrary to the official line from Ottawa, American delegations have visited Canada and "outlined ways" for Canadian participation, while, again, "none of the options Washington is currently pursuing for BMD would require Canadian participation."* Nevertheless, in the summer of 2002, another U.S. delegation came to Ottawa

with a view to increasing political support and opening the door to potential industrial participation.†

After all,

The BMD program could present Canadian industry with significant commercial opportunities in strategic sectors.

And, remember this:

Washington, for the most part, is limiting the industrial benefits to those nations that actually endorse the concept of BMD politically.

Sound familiar? Is this not exactly the kind of inducement the U.S. government used to encourage Western support for involvement in Iraq? Now consider this:

A significant risk associated with BMD from the non-proliferation and disarmament perspective is its reinforcement of trends towards the weaponizing of outer space.

---

* According to James Hackett in the *Washington Times*, March 23, 2004, a large floating radar in the North Pacific "avoids the need for another country to approve a radar base" and "a second sea-based radar is to be added later, probably in the North Atlantic."

† The first visit to Ottawa of senior U.S. Defense Department officials soliciting government support for BMD came one year earlier, in the summer of 2001.

Moreover,

> BMD could also increase the risks of further proliferation of missile technologies and weapons of mass destruction. Competitor states could seek to overwhelm missile defences through qualitative and quantitative improvements to their missile fleets, or simply attempt to circumvent defences through aggressive exploitation of cruise missiles and Unmanned Aerial Vehicle technologies.

And, more recently, the U.S. Defense Department now admits that missile defence costs will be far higher than earlier estimates. One reason our own defence documents cite is work to develop

> a new platform for airborne laser, plus a new multipurpose "kill vehicle" and new satellites.
>
> Some observers fear that BMD could accelerate . . . nuclear missile deployments, fuelling an arms race that could have an impact on [text blanked out] tensions.

And, in conclusion, to repeat,

> BMD is perhaps one of the most important security questions the government will have to consider.

Or, more certainly, *the* most important decision that the Canadian government will have to make relating to Canada's ability to control its own foreign and defence policies in the future.

LET'S NOT HAVE TOO MANY MEETINGS

The issue has nothing to do with going into space. . . . The present plan has nothing to do with the weaponizing of space.
— Bill Graham, February 2004

In the face of all the enormous amounts of official and scientific evidence to the contrary, one can only regard Bill Graham's comments on this topic with the utmost dismay. There are only a few possible conclusions. Either Graham is incompetent and well over his head in the foreign affairs portfolio, or he is very, very poorly briefed by his officials, or he has been intentionally misleading Canadians. For the reasons set out below, I do not believe the first two explanations.

In January, after a George W. Bush press conference, Dr. Laura Grego of the American Union of Concerned Scientists wrote:

One prominent goal of the new Bush initiative is to land the first human being on Mars. But the administration is also planning a first that has not been announced with a press conference: the first stationing of weapons in space.

The Bush administration began to press ahead with its military space plan at the very beginning of its term. And key parts are on fast track: the first prototype weapon is scheduled to be in orbit by 2007 or 2008. These plans are opposed by essentially the entire international community which rightly believes that going down this path will bring the world less security – not more.

Even Brian Mulroney, during the Cold War, understood the terrible dangers of Ronald Reagan's Star Wars plans. In a *Globe* op-ed piece Mulroney wrote:

> The Reagan administration ardently sought our support and counted on our participation. After a special cabinet and caucus meeting, I called President Reagan at Camp David and told him that my government had decided that participation was *not* in Canada's national interest.[*]

Contrast this with the words of Canada's next prime minister, Jean Chrétien, just before he stepped down late in 2003:

> We believe that missile defence has the potential to benefit Canada.

And Prime Minister Paul Martin? Was there ever any doubt about his intentions?

> I certainly don't want to see Canada isolated from any moves the United States might make to protect the continent.

And then, a bit later, in the most remarkable convoluted logic:

> I think our sovereignty depends on us being at the table when discussions are taking place.

Last November, in Toronto, Paul Martin said this:

---

[*] *Globe and Mail*, May 15, 2003.

Canada has to be at the table. We will fulfill our responsibility.

And, unafraid of frequent repetition, more recently Martin said:

> We're talking about the defence of North America . . . Canada has to
> be at the table . . . there's no doubt about security . . . We will exer-
> cise our responsibilities.

Now let's hear from a former defence minister, Liberal John McCallum,
the ex-Royal Bank economist, who somehow couldn't distinguish Vimy
from Vichy, and who was so shockingly ignorant of the story of Dieppe.[*]
For McCallum:

> We should get in there early. I hope not too many meetings will be
> necessary.

In January 2003, McCallum met with U.S. Secretary of Defense
Donald Rumsfeld in Washington and according to *Time* magazine

> *Time* has learned that during the session Canada effectively dropped
> its opposition to a Star Wars-type defense against ballistic missiles.

According to Liberal Senator Colin Kenny, chairman of the Standing
Senate Committee on National Security and Defence, "The reality is
that Canada is moving into a closer military relationship with the U.S."
Now here's Bill Graham, in an August 26, 2003 letter. Note this carefully.
Any decision we make will be made

> In a manner that respects Canada's long-standing policies on arms
> control and strategic stability, including our opposition to the
> weaponizing of space as articulated in the April 1999 Government
> Statement on Nuclear Disarmament and Non-proliferation.

---

[*] See McCallum's letter to the *National Post*, September 1, 2002.

The Nuclear Non-Proliferation Treaty forms the foundation of Canada's disarmament policy.

And then, remarkably and incomprehensibly

Current U.S. missile defence plans do not involve the weaponiza-tion of space.

Here's Bill Graham at the Couchiching conference in August 2003:

Our policies must respect Canada's long-standing policies on arms control and our leadership in developing the 2002 Hague Code of Conduct against ballistic missile proliferation and the control and development and proliferation of weapons of mass destruction.

Canada continues to take a leadership role in the conference on disarmament in Geneva, working with other governments to prevent the weaponizing of space.

Finally, here's a more recent quote from Bill Graham:

Canada is now quite prepared to examine participation in Bush's missile defence plan.

Next we come to long-time Paul Martin supporter, our former Minister of Defence David Pratt, the man who was previously Liberal Chairman of the House of Commons Defence Committee:

As a general principle, I'm in favour of the national missile defence ...

In May 2003, when Mary Lou Finlay questioned Pratt on the CBC radio program *As It Happens*, and when she suggested that Canada's partici-pation would undermine decades of our work for nuclear disarmament and set off a potentially deadly new arms race, Pratt said:

That's just Cold War thinking . . . we have to adapt to a new strategic environment.

In a January 2004 interview, Pratt claimed that the planned American National Missile Defense (NMD) program was only a modest program intended to intercept enemy ICBMs using ground-based technology, and if we don't take part Canada will have no say in what the Americans do.* Later in the month, Pratt attempted to calm Canadian fears with a remarkable claim that there was no need to worry, the American NMD program would not result in another arms race.

On January 15, 2004, Pratt exchanged letters with his U.S. counterparts to set the stage for final negotiations about Canada's participation. The letter makes it clear that negotiations between the two countries are already well advanced. An agreement is expected "in the coming months."

Pratt's letter to Donald Rumsfeld is not lacking in clarity as to intent. Canada intends

> to negotiate in the coming months a Missile Defence Framework Memorandum of Understanding (MOU) with the United States with the objective of including Canada as a participant in the current U.S. missile defence program . . . including increased government-to-government and industry-to-industry co-operation on missile defence that we should seek to foster between our countries.

Sounds a bit like we had already made up our minds, doesn't it?

The introduction of the letter, though, is once again bizarre in the extreme, and sounds remarkably similar to a George W. Bush speech.

---

* Pratt's claim that the U.S.'s NMD plans are only "a modest program" is in direct contradiction to the briefing documents quoted earlier. Pratt was defeated in the June 28 federal election.

> In light of the growing threat involving the proliferation of ballistic
> missiles and weapons of mass destruction, we should [co-operate]
> in missile defence, as an appropriate response to these new threats
> and as a useful complement to our non-proliferation efforts.

A first year political science student could handily demolish Pratt in a
debate based on this paragraph. As we will see, the American BMD plans
are *escalating* the production of weapons of mass destruction, including
the quality and quantity of ballistic missiles to deliver nuclear weapons,
and *ensuring* a growing proliferation of such weapons and delivery
systems. In other words, another terribly costly, incredibly foolish, and
horribly dangerous arms race.

If Pratt doesn't understand this, once again there can be only three
possibilities. Either he was very poorly briefed, which I do not believe
for a moment, or he is not very bright, or, he too was not being frank
with Canadians.

According to Donald Rumsfeld

> In light of the threat involving the proliferation of ballistic missiles,
> I agree that we should seek to expand our cooperation in the area of
> missile defense.

David Pratt made it clear that Canada intends ". . . to ensure the closest
possible involvement in the U.S. program." Well, it can't really be much
clearer than that, can it? According to an unnamed senior Canadian
official, "It is inching towards the inevitable" with the announcement
expected by most to come after the federal election.

So, what does all of this say about our current federal political leadership, when our prime minister, our minister of foreign affairs, and our
two former defence ministers, and almost all of the Liberal cabinet and
most of the caucus, plus the leader of the Conservative Party and virtually all of his caucus, are all in favour of dramatically reversing long-
standing, widely respected Canadian policies by rushing to climb on

board the American Star Wars plans, while blatantly ignoring or denying the inevitable dangerous consequences?

Privately, Bill Graham acknowledges that the reasoning of Canadian opponents of the NMD plans has "integrity," but the government will be making its decision based on "other factors." What other factors? We shall see shortly.

In Ottawa's direct public communications with Washington there's not a word about our opposition to the weaponization of space. We do say, however, that we recognize that the U.S. NMD system will evolve over time, and that our bilateral co-operation in this area should also evolve.

DON'T EVEN THINK ABOUT THINKING ABOUT IT

———————■———————

Canada has no choice but to co-operate fully with the United States on hemisphere defence . . .
— Historian Jack Granatstein, June 2002

In my last book, *The Vanishing Country*, I wrote at some length about the widening gap between the wishes of the powerful and influential radical-Right plutocracy in Canada, and the values and goals of the vast majority of Canadians.

In the debate about Canada's participation in the American BMD plans, the gulf between the two camps is readily discernible. Later we'll see how most Canadians feel about some of the issues discussed in this book. But first, let's look briefly at the pressures being brought to bear for Canada to become part of the U.S.'s plans. To begin, let's look at our national newspapers.

We don't have to dwell on the *National Post* (which should change its name to the *American Post*). We know where it stands. Pretty well anything the Americans want will be just fine, and thank you very much for asking.

Now let's hear from one of the columnists at our other national newspaper. According to the right-wing and continentalist John Ibbitson of the *Globe and Mail*,

The arguments in favour of supporting missile defence are so formidable as to preclude rational objection.

So, there you have it. Don't even *think* about objecting. Or, put another
way, don't even think about thinking. Ibbitson has decided, and he
says

> Canada needs to tell the Americans we are willing to join them on
> missile defence. And the sooner the better.

According to big business in the form of the 150-member powerful
and influential Canadian Council of Chief Executives – the CCCE
(who brought us free trade as the Business Council on National Issues),
we should

> enhance the interoperability of Canadian and U.S. armed forces . . .
> including Canadian participation in a continental anti-ballistic
> missile system.

Where else is the pressure coming from? To begin, there's the influential
Canadian Defence Industries Association, which anticipates hundreds of
millions of dollars in contracts if Canada signs on to the NMD plan. Then
there's the equally influential Aerospace Industries Association of
Canada. In *The Hill Times* (June 2, 2003), Steven Staples of the Polaris
Institute wrote:

> Business groups have been campaigning for months to push the
> Liberals closer to the Bush administration on a range of issues –
> especially national missile defence. In the back rooms of the missile
> defence debate one might find many of the players who were behind
> the Canada–U.S. Free Trade Agreement and NAFTA.
>   The respected U.S. defence industry magazine *Defense News*
> revealed last summer that the U.S. Missile Defense Agency wanted

to "lure foreign firms with U.S. defense dollars and hope the con-tractors sway their governments to get on board."

And then, there's none other than the crew of colonial-minded bureau-crats at DFAIT, who have long been pushing for deeper integration with the U.S.

What about all the reports that the U.S. is not all that interested in Canada's participation? Tariq Rauf of the International Atomic Energy Agency writes:

> For the last several months press reports suggest that the Canadian military is coming under increased pressure from its U.S. counter-part to show greater support for NMD and to formally join the pro-gramme. Speaking in Calgary (Alberta) on 18 February 2000, the then U.S. Deputy Defense Secretary John Hamre noted that Canada and the U.S. were at an important pivot point in their relationship and that the pivot point would revolve around the issue of NMD. He stated that "I must tell you that we need the help of Canada for this . . . Canada needs to take the lead. I honestly believe in helping to communicate with the rest of the world why it is important to amend the ABM Treaty. If we fail to do it, I promise you we're not going to protect the United States . . . And we can do this, I hate to say, by ourselves. We'd rather not do it by ourselves."
>
> U.S. Vice-Admiral Herbert Browne, [Deputy Commander in charge, U.S. Space Command], told a briefing that if U.S. satellites detected a hostile missile headed for Ottawa we would have absolutely no obligation to defend Ottawa from attack if Canada is not part of an NMD system. He raised the possibility of an attacker shooting at Ottawa and then Detroit or another U.S. city. If the U.S. used up all its available missile interceptors protecting Ottawa and could not defend U.S. targets, he noted that Americans would say "that makes absolutely no sense." He added that Canada should participate by installing high-powered radar to help track incoming

missiles. Browne noted that, in many cases, hostile missiles would be engaged over Canadian air space even if they were aimed at U.S. rather than Canadian targets.*

It's hardly unexpected that the arrogant and intrusive U.S. Ambassador Paul Cellucci has met with the Canadian aerospace group and has made it clear that he expects Canada to join in on the U.S. missile program. And, it should come as no surprise that Paul Martin met with both Cellucci and the CCCE's chief continentalist Tom d'Aquino last January. In relation to U.S. defence policies such as the proposed integrated joint defence of North America, Ambassador Cellucci warns us that if Canada doesn't go along with U.S. requests

> The alternative . . . might be that we would have to tighten up the border between Canada and the United States.

Then we had another stern warning from the Washington Center for Strategic and International Studies that if Canada doesn't go along with the Pentagon and the American BMD plans, it could

> Kill its six-decades-old military partnership with the world's only superpower.

You know, like the partnership that saw the Americans indifferently sit back for three years before finally becoming involved in the First World War, and for over two years in the Second World War, while many tens of thousands of Canadians were killed fighting in Europe. But, times have changed. Our own Canadian military is now anxious to become involved in American plans. General Ray Henault, Chief of Canada's Defence Staff, is all in favour. He wants a dramatic expansion of

---

* Robert Harrison, writing in *Policy Options* in November 2003, said that "Many of the animations on the official Pentagon Web site show radar stations and interceptor missile sites located in a country that looks suspiciously like Canada . . ."

Canada–U.S. military co-operation and says Canada must be part of the NMD programs.*

While there have been some claims that the U.S. doesn't need or even want Canada's participation, such claims are contradicted by an abundance of persuasive evidence to the contrary, including more blatant warnings that Canada will pay if we don't join in. In *The Vanishing Country* I spelled out why Canada need not be overly concerned about American threats, and why we are not anywhere near as vulnerable as some of our own continentalist cowards would have us believe.† It's just too bad that some of our big-business corporate leaders don't have the backbone to tell rude jerks like Richard Perle where to go when he so offensively threatens them, as he did in Washington in 2003, when he told a visiting delegation of Canadian CEOs that "Canada had better realize in future where its interests lie." Most Canadians would have said, "Thank you very much, but it's certainly *not* with George W. Bush."

---

* June 2003.

† *The Vanishing Country*, McClelland & Stewart Ltd., 2002, pages 390 to 397. For more on Paul Cellucci, see pages 66, 111, 116, and 393 in *The Vanishing Country*.

"How Could We Possibly Go Along?"

———————————

"Benign neglect from a majority of Canadians may be the realistic outcome of a well-executed communications program."
— Confidential memorandum, PMO, 1985

What do you think?

Should there have been an informed national debate about Canadian participation in the NMD program *before* such an important decision was made? Were Canadians given enough information by our government to make an informed judgment? And what should we make of John McCallum's statement that he hoped not too many meetings would be necessary before a decision was made?

Also, if we are to spend billions of dollars, or even only hundreds of millions, on our role in the missile program, what are the implications for health care funding, for education, for child poverty in Canada?

Since detailed discussions with U.S. officials have been going on now for four years, why have Canadians been told so little?* Has the Martin

---

* In a news release January 15, 2004, the Department of Foreign Affairs and International Trade (DFAIT) told us that "Canada and the United States established a BMD Bilateral Information Sharing Working Group that has met twice a year since 2000. In addition, Canada placed a Canadian Forces Liaison Officer with the U.S. Missile Defense Agency in early 2001 for the purpose of supporting the ongoing consultation and information exchange process."

government policy been to deliberately keep Canadians in the dark? It certainly seems this way. And, if this is the case, is it because confidential government polls show that those Canadians who do understand the implications are overwhelmingly opposed to Canadian participation?

Obviously the repeated misleading government claims that it had not yet made up its mind were directly tied to Paul Martin's desire to ensure that the American Star Wars plan did not become a major election issue. Walk down main street and ask people if any of them have ever heard Martin or Stephen Harper explain the ramifications of the weaponizing of space, the dangers of nuclear proliferation and renewed testing, the implications of a rapid increase in the deployment of weapons of mass destruction. And what about Canada's ability to chart its own foreign and defence policies in the future? Let's for a moment go back to September 1985 when

> A confidential memo leaked from the Prime Minister's Office showed just how honest and forthright Brian Mulroney intended to be with the people who had elected him to the nation's highest post: "The strategy should rely less on educating the general public than on getting across the message that the trade initiative is a good idea. In other words a selling job. It is likely that the higher the profile the issue attains, the lower the degree of public approval will be. Benign neglect from a majority of Canadians may be the realistic outcome of a well-executed communications program."*

Has a similar strategy been implemented in Martin's PMO? It certainly seems that way. Whatever we have been getting from Ottawa seems to fly in the face of all logic and an abundance of contrary evidence. Just as the Bush government lied to Americans and the world about Iraq, is it not increasingly evident that the government of Canada has been intentionally misleading Canadians about one of the most important decisions in our nation's history?

---

* *The Betrayal of Canada*, Stoddart, 1991.

Ottawa journalist Clyde Sanger (who writes about Canada for *The Economist*) reviewed Douglas Roche's latest book, *The Human Right to Peace*,[*] in the December 2003 edition of the *Literary Review of Canada*. Sanger writes that Roche's book

> describes a world . . . where certain governments are stunningly wrong-headed in their priorities and are lying to their people – most recently about Iraq, but more broadly about nuclear weapons.

Roche makes one of the absolutely key points in any discussion about Bush's plans. I hope you will read the following paragraph twice.

> Do not be taken in by fraudulent claims that this is about the defence of North America. It is about U.S. military control of space. It *is* about the Bush administration turning its back on the international legal system and the attempt by the U.S. to dominate world events.

I hope you will remember these words from Canada's widely respected former ambassador for disarmament whenever you hear or read Paul Martin, Bill Graham, or Stephen Harper on the subject.

Now let's hear from the long-time Liberal Member of Parliament from Toronto, John Godfrey, who has toiled patiently on the back-benches since he was elected in 1993. Here is what Godfrey wrote about Bush's NMD plans in the *Globe and Mail before* he was appointed Parliamentary Secretary to the Prime Minister by Paul Martin in December 2003.

> For Canada to embrace this plan for NMD is for us to accept two hard truths: that nuclear proliferation is now out of control in the world; and that the Bush doctrine of unilateralism, pre-emption, and military domination announced last September must not be challenged.

---

[*] Novalis, 2003.

Canada would be explicitly repudiating 50 years of painstaking work in arms control and an abiding belief that war should always be the last option.

We are also told that it is better to be inside the tent than out, that we can only have influence with the Americans by going along with them this time and gaining "a place at the table." But, the Bush doctrine makes no allowance for disagreement, influence or even nuanced differences – there is no table to sit down at!

How, on the grounds of sovereignty, self-interest or international morality could we possibly go along?[*]

In contrast, here's former defence minister Pratt in the House of Commons: "The . . . reason Canada is proceeding with negotiations . . . is to safeguard our sovereignty."

In early February, in what I promised would be a private conversation, I talked to a prominent Liberal MP in Ottawa. He has been a consistent, articulate, and staunch opponent of the NMD plans. But, he's now also close to Paul Martin. I asked the MP what possible reasons there could be for Canada signing on. Here's what he said, after what seemed to be an awkward pause:

The only thing that makes any sense is improving Canada–U.S. relations. It will be seen to be a test of loyalty.

So much for principles. So much for Canada's role in promoting peace and disarmament. So much for morality and valuing human life.

How could we possibly go along? For at least two years Paul Martin made it very clear that he wanted Canada to move closer to the United States. He wanted even more integration, more harmonization, and more shared policies, including military and defence policies. In other words, all the things that Brian Mulroney and Stephen Harper have also long wanted.

---

[*] *Globe and Mail*, May 12, 2003.

Then there's Iraq. Here's Nobel laureate John Polanyi in the *Globe and Mail* on May 7, 2003:

> The Canadian government, having held back from President George W. Bush's rush to war in Iraq, appears likely to join his rush to missile defence.

And a few days later, here's NDP MP Bill Blaikie in the House of Commons:

> I firmly believe, as many do, that our rush to judgement is not due to some American timetable, but is due to an overzealous desire on the part of the government to make up for the decision that was taken with respect to Canadian non-participation in the war in Iraq.*

Here's a report of comments by former foreign affairs minister Lloyd Axworthy reported in the *Globe* earlier this year:

> Lloyd Axworthy recently said his former Liberal colleagues are trying to atone to Washington for the government's failure to support the U.S. invasion of Iraq last year.†

And former MP and cabinet minister Sheila Copps made a similar point in the House of Commons:

> Madam chair, one of the most potentially dangerous aspects of this discussion is the potential on the part of Canada that this is our *mea culpa* for Iraq, that somehow because as a country we chose to exercise our sovereign decision on Iraq, a decision that I think was

---

* *Globe and Mail*, May 15, 2003.

† February 17, 2004.

widely supported around the world but a decision that was not very popular south of the border, that we are limiting our choices for the future.[*]

I believe that one of the reasons the Department of National Defence has been very anxiously pursuing this agenda is because it sees it as a way back into the hearts of their American allies.

Earlier this year, in George Melnyk's new collection, *Canada and the New American Empire*, I wrote

The Chrétien government's decision not to join the American invasion of Iraq surprised and pleased most Canadians. Since the invasion, public opinion polls have consistently shown the majority of Canadians supported the government's decision and in recent months that support has grown even stronger.

As elsewhere, including in the United States, more and more the invasion is seen as an illegal and tragic imperialistic blunder which is well on the way to producing a Vietnam-like quagmire while generating widespread hatred and increasing terrorism around the world, with more and worse certain to come in the future.

The pressure on the Chrétien government to join George W. Bush's ill-advised "pre-emptive" aggression was unrelenting. The threats from the likes of U.S. ambassadors Paul Cellucci and Gordon Giffin, and [national security adviser] Condoleezza Rice were blunt and arrogant. Canada was expected to join in and it would be "unthinkable" if we did not. *Time* magazine said Canada could pay a hefty price for the government's anti-war stance.

The public opinion polls continue to be revealing. Most Canadians want us to be independent of American domination, want us to support multilateralism, want us to preserve our own standards, values and quality of life.

---

[*] Spoken a few days before the terrible train bombing in Spain in March.

Yet whatever pride we can take in relation to our principled decision re Iraq, our government will quickly trample in their uncompromising rush to join Bush's National Missile Defense plan, to integrate our military with the U.S. military, to join in behind "the perimeter," while selling off even more of the ownership and control of our country.

If Canada abandons its long-standing opposition to the weaponizing of space by supporting the NMD, and if we further integrate our military with the U.S. military, any proud remnant of our foreign policy legacy will be swept down the drain forever.

This said, two-thirds of Canadians say that maintaining the sovereignty of Canada is the most important challenge facing our country, only 8 per cent want us to become more like the United States, and three in five say that we are losing our independence from the U.S., while 89 per cent say that the quality of life is better in Canada than it is in the U.S.

Yet with the Paul Martin government, we're going to be heading to even more integration, more harmonization, and more Americanizing policies, standards and values.

How could we possibly go along? Today, as I'm writing these words, a new Ipsos-Reid poll shows that 67 per cent of adult Canadians agree with the statement that George W. Bush "knowingly lied to the world to justify his war with Iraq," and in a CBC poll 79 per cent said that Canada was right in not joining the U.S. invasion of Iraq. Now here's David Pratt in the House of Commons, February 17, 2004

Some would have Canadians believe that we proceeded with discussions on missile defence in an attempt to mend fences with the United States. This is patently false.

Okay, then one is forced to wonder *why*, in the face of such strong and consistent Canadian public opinion polls on the subject of Iraq, Paul Martin and his cabinet somehow have felt obliged to apologize for a clearly correct and overwhelmingly popular decision. As for the staunchly, eternally pro-American Stephen Harper, no further explanation is really required. For Harper, "We should have been there, standing shoulder to shoulder with our allies."*

Paul Heinbecker was formerly Canadian ambassador to the United Nations and is now director of the Laurier Centre for Global Relations, Governance and Policy at Wilfrid Laurier University. In a March *Globe and Mail* article, he wrote:

> Rarely in life is a decision so quickly and thoroughly vindicated as Canada's decision to opt out of the war in Iraq. A year later, the stated *causus belli* has evaporated. No weapons of mass destruction have been found, despite the best efforts of more than a thousand American weapons inspectors with free reign. No connection to al-Qaeda has been established. No persuasive argument endures about the urgency of the U.S. need to act.

And then, in a wonderful summary sentence,

> . . . going along has never made good public policy, or good politics, either.

---

* By July 2004, a CBS-*New York Times* poll showed that even in the U.S. a majority of Americans now say that the U.S. should not have invaded Iraq.

"A PANDEMIC OF INSECURITY":
ESCALATION, DESTABILIZATION, PROLIFERATION

At the UN *conference on the Non-Proliferation Treaty, there was broad condemnation of the* BMD *on the grounds that it would undermine decades of arms control agreements and provoke a new weapons race.*

— Noam Chomsky, 2001

From Bill Graham in the House of Commons we learned that

I have been very proud to stand with my colleague Colin Powell at international meetings and say that Canada is with the United States in trying to ensure that non-proliferation takes place.

Canada is with the United States as we go out into the world to make it a safer place.*

Now here is Frank P. Harvey, Director of the Centre for Foreign Policy Studies at Dalhousie University, in a *Globe and Mail* commentary:

---

* *Hansard*, February 19, 2004.

Concerns about a new arms race proved to be exaggerated, as did ominous predictions about proliferation by Russia and China.*

While Graham has been very proud to stand with Colin Powell, and Harvey believes concerns about an arms race and proliferation are exaggerated, most of the world thinks otherwise.

No proliferation? No arms race? A safer place? How incredibly bizarre! Michael Costello, a former secretary of the Australian Department of Foreign Affairs and Trade, writes in *The Australian*:

> If you were Russia and China and faced a crisis with the U.S., and you thought the latter's national missile defence system could take out a large number of your warheads, the pressure would be on you to use them in pre-emptive strikes. And who can say there won't be another crisis of the 1962 Cuban variety, or like the little-known one that erupted in 1983 between the Soviet Union and the U.S.? Just think about Taiwan.
>
> If the U.S. goes down this path, the only reasonable response for China would be to increase the number of intercontinental ballistic and nuclear warheads by a factor of 10 – that is, instead of 200 warheads it will have 2,000. China will build up its submarine-launched ballistic missile capability and it will develop an anti-satellite program to target U.S. satellites.
>
> In turn, India's only reasonable response to a Chinese buildup would be to vastly expand its own nuclear arsenal. And Pakistan will see itself as having no choice but to follow suit.
>
> In any crisis with the U.S., the NMD system will result in immense pressure on Russia and China to launch their nuclear missiles pre-emptively.†

---

* *Globe and Mail*, February 25, 2004.

† *The Australian*, January 23, 2004. (China already has almost 450 warheads.)

How has Russia reacted to American plans? Not well known is the fact that Russian leaders made it clear to both the Chrétien and Martin governments that they are appalled by the American BMD plans, and that they fervently hoped that Canada would tell the Americans and the rest of the world that we will not participate. In response to Canadian suggestions that Canada will join in as long as the system remains air- and sea-based, and will withdraw if the Americans proceed with the weaponizing of space, the word "preposterous" was employed several times. "Do you think for a moment that having signed on, the Americans will let you withdraw? To say down the road that you didn't know that they were planning weapons in space will be beyond all credibility."

In 2000, just before Christmas, President Vladimir Putin paid a three-day visit to Ottawa and the recently re-elected Prime Minister Jean Chrétien. A major theme of the meeting was U.S. plans to proceed with the National Missile Defense system, and Moscow's strong support for the Anti-Ballistic Missile Treaty that the Bush government was threatening to walk away from. Putin's main goal in Ottawa was to enlist Chrétien's opposition to the American plans. He came away with nothing in the way of tangible results.

A few days later, French President Jacques Chirac visited Ottawa and warned that if the Bush administration went ahead with the NMD system, it could well lead to a resurgence of nuclear proliferation.*

Despite the nonsense from the Canadian government to the contrary, George W. Bush's Star Wars plans, make no mistake about it, are *already* leading to massive military destabilization, rapidly expanding nuclear proliferation, with a huge escalation in the potential for disastrous nuclear confrontation. Here again are the words of Mohamed ElBaradei

> The very existence of nuclear weapons gives rise to the pursuit of them. They are seen as a source of global influence, and are valued

---

* United Press International, December 19, 2000.

for their perceived deterrent effect. And as long as some countries possess them (or are protected by them in alliances) and others do not, this asymmetry breeds chronic global insecurity.*

From the *Los Angeles Times*:

If the missile defense system is built, the CIA believes China would install multiple independent warheads on its missiles in an effort to overwhelm any missile shield.

Moreover, U.S. intelligence officials say that

Russia and China would increase proliferation, including selling countermeasures for sure to such nations as Korea and Iran.†

And, when India sees a Chinese buildup, it too will increase its arsenal, with Pakistan following in tandem. Former American national security advisor Brent Scowcroft says

We ought to think about whether we want the Chinese to change their very minimalist strategy, and what the consequences would be.

The response from China looks ominous. Here is Dr. Li Bin, director of the Arms Control Program, Institute of International Studies, Tsinghua University, Beijing:

The planned deployment of the U.S. National Missile Defense (NMD) system is viewed by China as a threat to its national security and a destabilizing initiative . . . NMD deployment would disturb the strategic stability between China and the USA and increase the risk of conflict . . . The NMD will become a new and

---

* *The Economist*, October 18, 2003.

† *Los Angeles Times*, May 19, 2000.

serious obstacle that blocks China from considering joining global nuclear reduction efforts.[*]

A report by the Republican Policy Committee of the U.S. Senate (March 22, 2004) states that the Department of Defense concludes that

> Beijing has greatly expanded its arsenal of increasingly accurate and lethal ballistic missiles and long-range strike aircraft that are ready for immediate application should the [People's Liberation Army] be called upon to conduct war before its modernization aspirations are fully realized. This expansion includes replacement of its current intercontinental ballistic missiles.

For those who remember the Japan–U.S. trade origins of the Second World War in the Pacific, the recent news that China is increasingly becoming a scapegoat in Washington is ominous. China now has a $125-billion annual trade surplus[†] with the U.S., and, as Barry McKenna has reported from Washington

> The pressure on the Bush administration to take action against China is intensifying. It's coming from workers, Congress, businesses and ordinary Americans.[**]

In a top secret report obtained by the *Los Angeles Times*, U.S. defence officials say this about missile defence:

> There are more accurate, more reliable, and much cheaper ways of delivering chemical, biological, or nuclear weapons. These include ship-launched missiles, suitcase bombs, and other covert means.

---

[*] Jane's International Security News.htm, March 7, 2001.

[†] Of course much of this deficit is the result of U.S. firms manufacturing in China and shipping finished products or parts and components back to the U.S.

[**] *Globe and Mail*, March 19, 2004.

In all of this, forget about the Non-Proliferation Treaty, and its "unequivocal undertaking" in 2000 that all countries, including Russia and the U.S., agree to the total elimination of their nuclear weapons. And forget for sure the Bush–Putin summit of 2002, where both countries pledged a two-thirds reduction in their nuclear weapons over the next ten years. As Douglas Roche has pointed out, these countries, along with the United Kingdom, France, and China "have been warned time and time again that their refusal to honour their NPT obligations is leading to the complete breakdown of the agreement."

The latest U.S. defence budget is staggering – an unprecedented $447 billion with another $50 billion likely to be requested by the Pentagon later this year. It includes money for the development of new "usable" nuclear weapons that will produce massive collateral damage but will nevertheless be intended to somehow blur the distinction between conventional and nuclear war. The current U.S. budget for nuclear weapons, in real terms, is almost 40 per cent more than in any of the Cold War years.

Without a shadow of a doubt, the U.S. plans are already triggering a massive destabilization and a major buildup of nuclear arms and better, quicker methods to deliver them. *Instead of contributing to security, security is being seriously diminished.* Arms control and non-proliferation and no-testing agreements have been or will be abandoned. China will install many more land-based and submarine-launched multiple, independent nuclear warheads, multiple effective new decoys and other means to mislead U.S. radar, and along with North Korea and Russia, will develop a new, more deadly generation of missiles, land-based and sea-based, and many more deadly, sea-launched cruise missiles that the NMD system will be completely powerless to counter.

It's remarkable that in the "secret" and "confidential" defence department briefing documents that I referred to earlier, the two authors, a senior policy officer* and an assistant deputy minister,† downplay any

---

* Corey Michael Dvorkin.

† Kenneth J. Calder.

need for concern about Russia's reaction to Bush's NMD plans, saying that the response of both Russia and China "has been modest" and "muted" and "frictions with Russia have not emerged" as a result of BMD plans, and "Russian concerns over strategic stability appear largely to have been addressed."

This is nothing but 100 per cent pure nonsense. Don't believe any of it for a minute. Last November, a senior Russian military official, Col-Gen. Yuri Baluyevsky, first deputy chief of the armed forces general staff, warned that Russia would now have no alternative but to develop more nuclear weapons and more effective delivery systems if the U.S. continues with its plans.

> We are witnessing that nuclear weapons, which have served as a political deterrent, are being transformed into a battlefield instrument . . . I believe we must review our nuclear strategy.
>
>   We are asking WHY? There is no Warsaw Pact, and Russian policies are different from Cold War policies.*

Another senior Russian official said it's all

> Highly destabilizing . . . It's very scary, extremely scary.

More recently, Russian President Vladimir Putin announced that Russia is now planning "weapons of the new generation," and, in Ernie Regehr's words

> Russia is also beginning to mimic the U.S. declaration of its prerogative to use small nuclear weapons pre-emptively

while China will be tripling its nuclear-armed ICBMs by 2010 and in recent years its overall military spending has grown by double-digit percentages. For Regehr

---

* Associated Press, Moscow, November 26, 2003.

The arms race and strategic competition between major powers were not supposed to be part of the post-Cold War. The more credible the defence, the more it encourages the expansion of a credible threat, thus undermining the non-proliferation effort.

Russia's apparently sanguine approach to U.S. BMD is built on its unambiguous commitment to ensuring that its offensive capacity will always be able to overwhelm any defence effort that the U.S. tries to develop.

That means a clear floor on its nuclear reductions, contrary to its obligations under the Non-Proliferation Treaty.

The very pursuit of BMD undermines non-proliferation efforts, thus helping to create conditions under which BMD cannot be successful – it is the classic lose-lose scenario.[*]

In the words of John Polanyi

The pursuit of security through unbridled armament will have led to a pandemic of insecurity.

Last year, Russia began to deploy more SS-19 ICBMs equipped with MIRV (multiple independently-targeted re-entry vehicle) warheads. Vladimir Putin said that "their combat potential, including penetrating any missile defence systems, is without peer."[†] Putin says Russia has no choice. "As other countries increase the number and quality of their arms and military potential, then Russia will also need to ensure it has a new generation of arms and technology."

The Bulletin of the Atomic Scientists makes what should be, but obviously isn't, a seminal point:

Missile defense systems also indirectly threaten populations. The 1960s Soviet ABM system was intended to protect Moscow against

---

[*] Regehr, ibid.

[†] www.thebulletin.org/issues/2004

nuclear attacks, but rather than shielding Moscow from nuclear peril, the system in fact had the opposite effect of attracting nuclear warheads. An American commander stated: "We must have targeted Moscow with 400 weapons."

The *Bulletin* continues

The dynamics of nuclear competition and the history of the U.S. targeting of the Soviet system remind us that missile defense systems are potent drivers of offensive nuclear response. The missile defense that the Bush administration is building will be no exception and it will certainly attract nuclear targeting from the start.[*]

Putin says Russia has no choice. "As other countries increase the number and quality of their arms and military potential, then Russia will also need to ensure it has a new generation of arms and technology."

On January 30, 2004, the Associated Press reported from Moscow that Russia's approach is no longer "sanguine."

Russia's nuclear forces reportedly are preparing their largest maneuvers in two decades, an exercise involving the test-firing of missiles and flights by dozens of bombers in a massive simulation of an all-out nuclear war.

President Vladimir Putin is expected to personally oversee the maneuvers. . . .

The exercise . . . would closely resemble a 1982 Soviet exercise dubbed the "seven-hour nuclear war" that put the West on edge.[†]

---

[*] Charley Reese has pointed out that more than half of the U.S. population lives in seventy-five metropolitan areas which would be targets in a nuclear war. "The Russians could put 10 nuclear warheads on each of those targets and still have many, many hundreds of warheads left." (www.antiwar.com, February 7, 2004)

[†] *Washington Times*, January 30, 2004.

The Economist puts it well:

> More and more the U.S. nuclear weapons are being considered as part of the military arsenal, not deterrent weapons to be employed as a last resort. It makes no sense for the country with easily the most powerful military in the world to provide potential enemies with the excuses to develop and use nuclear arms as a response ... How do you tell others to abide by the NPT if you go on building newer and more bombs? Moreover, there is now increasing pressure in the U.S. for a resumption of testing. All in all, an increasingly dangerous path.

Western press reports of the Russian military exercises jubilantly reported under the headline "Putin's play for strength misfires,"* that two ICBMs failed, and made fun of Putin for donning a naval officers uniform to board the nuclear submarine *Arkhangelsk.* (Sound familiar?)

Of more importance was Putin's promise to make sure that Russia's nuclear offensive capacity was strengthened, and the blunt comments by Colonel General Baluyevsky that Russia's future buildup was prompted by concerns about American policies. Remarkably, a *Globe and Mail* editorial chose to advise that

> This is not the right signal [for Russia] to be sending to prospective allies, nervous neighbours or even his own citizens.†

One wonders if any thought was given by the editorial writer to the huge actual and planned U.S. military buildup that prompted the Russian tests and comments. (The U.S. military budget is between six and seven times that of Russia's.)

On February 18, while admitting that one missile self-destructed after ninety-eight seconds of flight, Russia denied press reports of the

---

* *National Post,* February 18, 2004.

† *Globe and Mail,* February 18, 2004.

complete failure of its ballistic missile launches. The next day President Putin announced that Russia is developing new "technical weapons" that will travel "at supersonic speed,"[*] and *China View* reported that

> Russian President Vladimir Putin said Wednesday that his country may begin building its own missile defense system and the military will be equipped with strategic weapons. . . .
>
> "Russia must work for a breakthrough in developing a new generation of defense hardware" [and because] other countries are increasing their military potential qualitatively and quantitatively "Russia should have a military potential to counteract modern threats" according to the Itar-Tass news agency. . . .
>
> Putin did not elaborate on the new strategic weapons, only saying that they will be "capable of striking targets deep inside continents at hypersonic speed."[†] Military experts refer to a new manoeuvrable high-speed warhead resembling a space cruise missile.

Did anyone, anywhere, except Bill Graham, David Pratt, and Stephen Harper and friends *really* doubt for a single moment that George W. Bush and Donald Rumsfeld would precipitate a massive new arms race? On February 19, 2004, *Asia Times Online* carried a lengthy and chilling report of changes in Russian policy as a result of U.S. moves. Dozens of previously stored multi-warhead SS-19 ICBMs are being made combat-ready. SS-24 rail-mobile missiles with ten warheads each and a yield of 550 kilotons were being placed on alert, and Russia's three missile armies and sixteen divisions with a total of 3,159 warheads have been told that Russia now "retains the right to launch a pre-emptive strike." Defense Minister Sergei Ivanov warned that Russia will be forced to alter its nuclear policies if emerging threats from the U.S. continue. The same day, the Associated Press reported from Moscow that

---

[*] *The Russian Journal*, February 19, 2004.

[†] Xinhua News Agency, February 19, 2004.

Russia has successfully tested a hypersonic anti-Star Wars weapon capable of penetrating any prospective missile shield. . . .

The prototype weapon proved it could manoeuvre so quickly as to make "any missile defense useless," Col-Gen Yuri Baluyevsky, the first deputy chief of the General Staff of the Russian armed forces, told a news conference.

He said that the prototype of a new hypersonic vehicle had proved its ability to manoeuvre while in orbit, thereby making it able to dodge an enemy's missile shield. . . .

Baluyevsky's comment followed a statement by President Vladimir Putin . . . that Russia could build new strategic weapons that would be unrivaled in the world.*

Writing in *New York Press*, American journalist and commentator Alexander Zaitchik says

When the U.S.S.R. collapsed, American public interest in nuclear weapons disappeared under the rubble. People boxed up their fears and hauled them down to the basements of their souls like some hideous secret, never to be looked upon again. Thirteen years later, we're still willful strangers to thermonuclear dread, carrying on as if the nuclear stockpiles amassed during the Cold War had all been converted into solar panels and parakeet swings under Boris Yeltsin's kindly gaze.

Of course, they weren't. Most of those warheads are still live, still scattered under prairies, under seas, on roving flatbed trucks, ready to launch at a moment's notice. Right now, thousands of them are aimed at you, your family and your favorite television and sports personalities.

Against a backdrop of nuclear proliferation, both Russia and the U.S. continue to maintain and refine their own arsenals. They are also lowering the thresholds for their use. As Washington pushes

---

* *Globe and Mail*, February 19, 2004.

forward with missile defense and a bonus round of NATO expansion, Russian generals are bristling, while Russia's command and control system continues to deteriorate, increasing the chance that misjudgment, error or sabotage could trigger a missile launch against, say, New York City, which is targeted for a couple hundred megatons. According to those analysts who never took their eyes off the nuclear threat, the danger of a missile exchange between U.S. and Russia is actually greater today than during the more stable periods of the Cold War.[*]

Keep these words in mind when you read the remarkable story on the last four pages of this book.

According to General Baluyevsky, Russia has no alternative but to respond to U.S. NMD plans and the so-called precision-guided bunker busters which were proposed in Bush's latest budget request to Congress.[†]

> The U.S. is making nuclear weapons an instrument of solving military tasks while lowering the threshold of nuclear weapons use. Shouldn't we react to that?

There are new signs that U.S.–Russian relations are deteriorating, and not just over the Bush missile plans. Recent tensions relating to oil, pipeline routes, NATO expansion, the Caucasus, and central Asia have been chilling for anyone familiar with the bilateral discussions. Zaitchik continues:

> Neither Russia nor the U.S. ever stopped viewing preparation for war against the other as the central organizing principle of its nuclear policy . . . This means that American and Russian rocket-mounted nuclear weapons remain armed, fueled, loaded and kept at hair-trigger readiness 24 hours a day, 365 days a year.

---

[*] New York Press, vol. 17, issue 7.

[†] On June 25, 2004, the House of Representatives cut funding for the new bunker busters, but the Senate was expected to reinstate some portion of the funding in the fall.

Today, the Pentagon's clearly articulated goal of "full spectrum dominance" is producing, according to Zaitchik, "hypersensitivity about U.S. intentions" and "paranoia and bitterness" that is being translated into policy.

> The declaration of American intent to "own" and weaponize space, the proposed building of a missile defence system and other high-tech weapons that threaten the effectiveness of Russia's nuclear deterrent . . . has sharpened tensions with Russia and increased the risk of nuclear war.
>
> One is forgiven for wondering if anybody at the Pentagon or the White House has any appreciation of how foreign threat perception can adversely affect U.S. national security.

For Zaitchik,

> . . . there is in this country no significant public discussion about nuclear policy or the massive arsenals on both sides of the old Cold War divide.
>
> The U.S. nuclear arsenal is today being upgraded and expanded, keeping government scientists and engineers busy designing new generations and classes of missiles. Plans are being discussed for the weaponization of space and funding is slated for new plutonium "pit" factories.[*]
>
> In short, America's nuclear weapons program is back to mid-1980s levels of funding and activity, while public interest is stuck at mid-1990s levels.
>
> At the same time, a political sea change in nuclear thinking has been occurring in Washington, where it was once universally accepted that nuclear weapons were horrible things and that

---

[*] Plutonium pits are the essential cores of nuclear weapons. They are contained in corrosion-resistant metal surrounded by powerful chemical explosives. Upon detonation, a fission chain reaction occurs. The U.S. is now planning to produce "between 125 and 450 pits annually" according to the Union of Concerned Scientists.

disarmament was a noble, if distant goal. This was implicit in our signing of the Non-Proliferation Treaty, which paid lip service to the promise of eventual major power disarmament.

No more. For today's right wing, there is no such thing as a bad weapon – there are only bad *countries*. This thinking is represented starkly in American threats to use nukes against non-nuclear enemies, as stated in 2002's official Nuclear Posture Review.

Even if the current administration can restrain itself from acting on this new philosophy, such thinking could already be percolating down through the defense establishment. At a conference last month sponsored by the Nuclear Policy Research Institute, General Charles Horner of the U.S. Air Force warned of "a danger of creating a generation in the military that sees nuclear weapons as an acceptable form of warfare."

That the nuclear firewall is being lowered even before it is breached is evident in Russia's evolving nuclear doctrine as well. The Russians have made it clear that they now reserve the right to use nuclear weapons even in the face of conventional threats. This is a post-Cold War development for both countries.

In January 2003, the Union of Concerned Scientists warned that

The administration's policies regarding America's own nuclear weapons have systematically undercut the Nuclear Non-Proliferation Treaty (NPT), which has for 33 years defined the only internationally accepted barrier to nuclear proliferation.

The administration's foreign and defense policies convey a clear message to present and future adversaries of the United States: spare no effort to acquire nuclear weapons!

In the arms reduction negotiations between Presidents Bush and Putin, the administration insisted on maintaining nuclear forces of Cold War dimensions.

The president's desire for a free hand to develop and test new weapons has led the administration to abandon the U.S. obligation to ratify the Comprehensive Test Ban Treaty.

By displaying such an addiction to nuclear weapons while possessing the world's most powerful conventional forces, the administration is constructing the strongest imaginable rationale for other countries to acquire nuclear weapons. The administration should not have been surprised that North Korea has heard its message, especially after President Bush asserted that the United States has the right – in peacetime and on its own authority – to use all means at its disposal to prevent states from acquiring nuclear weapons.

Zaitchik concludes:

Any Democrat that replaces Bush in 2004 will have his hands full just rolling back the minute hand on the nuclear clock to where it stood in 2000. Pushing it back further will be a more difficult project still, but that doing so is an urgent and front-burner task there can be no doubt. In averting nuclear disaster after the Cold War, we've all been very lucky. But the thing about luck is, it eventually runs out.

While Bill Graham stands fast with his colleague Colin Powell to ensure that "the world will be a safer place," and is somehow confident that we need not worry about an arms race, all the abundant evidence makes him appear extraordinarily obtuse. French President Jacques Chirac says that the American missile defence plans "cannot fail to relaunch the arms race in the world,"* and senior Russian officials are promising an "asymmetrical response" to the U.S. nuclear buildup.

The Chinese have made it clear that they regard American NMD plans as seriously undermining their deterrent, while the Russians are again

---

* www.wcpeace.org/bmd.htm

test-firing intercontinental ballistic missiles from both land and sea in preparation for the possibility of an all-out nuclear war with the United States.

An out-of-control arms race is a terrible danger to Canada and to all Canadians, but the Liberal government is bent on officially becoming part of the American plans that are causing the rapidly growing Russian and Chinese anxiety. Yet contrary to all logic, in a letter to Canadian physicists (March 11, 2004) Paul Martin, preparing to justify an announcement of Canada's participation in the NMD system, says:

> The government of Canada believes that it is our fundamental responsibility to look into options that could enhance the safety and security of Canadians.

And in an April 29, 2004 form letter, Bill Graham repeated exactly the same words, adding:

> It is our responsibility to ensure that Canada's national interests are protected . . . The government of Canada has also emphasized non-proliferation, arms control and disarmament as another aspect of our strategy to protect Canadians.

An escalating and terribly dangerous arms race is now in progress. Canadians who care about their future and the future of the world should view the policy pursued by Graham, and the prime minister, and Stephen Harper and his party, with the disdain it deserves.

SHIELD OF DREAMS:
WHY THE AMERICAN NATIONAL
MISSILE DEFENSE WON'T WORK

———■———

From the Reagan Strategic Defense Initiative (SDI) years to 2002, of the 96 missile defense tests, only two were claimed to be totally successful.

A group of U.S. scientists have criticized the National Missile Defense (NMD) programme, saying that no matter how much money the Department of Defense poured into it, the system would never work.

— www.Janes.com, June 19, 2000

Even the full National Missile Defense system would not be effective against an attacker using countermeasures. The system the Bush administration plans to deploy by 2004 will have essentially no defense capability.

— Union of Concerned Scientists

Sitting on my desk is a massive pile of press reports about "The Pentagon's Laughable Weapons Test" (Slate, June 20, 2003): "the Pentagon quietly announced it has suspended tests due to technological difficulties" (*Globe and Mail*, August 22, 2003), "Military Contractor Faked Tests: Millions Wasted" (nationalsecurity@taxpayer.net, March 14, 2000);

and many, many similar clippings and printouts announcing "another setback," "one more failure," "an engine malfunction," etc. The faked tests are interesting: A leading military contractor put a highly misleading gloss on results for a key component in the proposed National Missile Defense system.

> Dr. Nira Schwartz worked for TRW, a military contractor, helping design a computer program enabling missile interceptors to distinguish between incoming warheads and decoys. The program failed numerous tests. But when Dr. Schwartz requested her superiors communicate these problems to the federal government, she was fired.
>
> With more than $6.9 million doled out in campaign contributions during the 1997–98 election cycle from NMD contractors (Lockheed Martin, Boeing, TRW and Raytheon) some critics argue that campaign cash may drive the NMD debate.[*]

According to CNN:

> The Missile Defense Agency (MDA) conducted a missile defense test over Hawaii, and while the warhead did not strike the target, officials said they still considered the exercise a success.
>
> Chris Taylor, a MDA spokesman, said "we obviously don't know exactly what went wrong." (Raytheon Missile Systems is the prime contractor.)
>
> According to Senators Carl Levin of Michigan and Jack Reed of Rhode Island, the MDA had "immature technology and limited testing." Levin said a General Accounting Office report showed that the planned missile defense system will not be fully tested or proven to work under realistic conditions.[†]

---

[*] *Common Dreams*, May 15, 2002.

[†] June 19, 2003.

Salon carried this wonderful story by columnist Joe Conason in July 2001:

> The Pentagon and the Bush administration are determined to sell the American people a national missile defense system that will probably increase tensions with allies and adversaries and will surely cost more that $100 billion. Their latest marketing exercise took place on the evening of July 14, when a "kill vehicle" launched from the Kwajalein Atoll in the Pacific smashed into a rocket sent up from Vandenberg Air Force Base in California.
>
> Precisely according to plan, the target was instantly vaporized on impact – and along with it, or so the Pentagon's uniformed salesmen hoped, the perennial concern that missile defense won't work. With the co-operation of major news organizations and conservative pundits, that test provided an enormous propaganda boost to the Bush proposal, which conveniently enough had been brought up to Capital Hill by Defense Department officials just two days earlier.
>
> There was only one thing that all the happy salesmen forgot to mention about the latest test drive. The rocket fired from Vandenberg was carrying a global positioning satellite beacon that guided the kill vehicle toward it. In other words it would be fair to say that the $100 million test was rigged.

As indicated at the beginning of this chapter, from the Reagan SDI years to 2002, of the ninety-six U.S. missile defence tests, only two were claimed to be totally successful. But even the "successful" results have been criticized as unrepresentative of what would happen in a real missile attack. Even Pentagon officials themselves described the tests as "highly scripted" under ideal conditions. In any event, two "successful" hits out of ninety-six tests is hardly reassuring when any attack from the likes of Russia or China would include huge numbers of warheads, decoys, and other protective devices.

As early as June of 2000

AUGUSTANA LIBRARY
UNIVERSITY OF ALBERTA

A group of U.S. scientists has criticized the National Missile
Defense (NMD) programme, saying that no matter how much
money the Department of Defense poured into it, the system would
never work.*

About the same time, the U.S.-based Union of Concerned Scientists and
the MIT Security Studies Program came to the conclusion that

Even the full National Missile Defense system would not be effective
against an attacker using countermeasures.

After very carefully studying the Pentagon's plans, the Union of Concerned Scientists pointed out that the technology needed for an
effective system still doesn't exist:

And even if the technology worked perfectly, the systems being
deployed are vulnerable to countermeasures that are easier to build
than the long-range missile on which they would be placed. This
problem contributed to President Clinton's 2000 decision not to
deploy the system the Bush administration is now fielding.

Just before the election of George W. Bush, Clinton told Americans

I simply cannot conclude with the information I have today that
we have enough confidence in the technology, and the operational
effectiveness of the entire NMD system, to move forward to
deployment.†

In early 2001, Lisbeth Gronlund of MIT and a member of the board of
the *Bulletin of the Atomic Scientists*, wrote to newly elected President
George W. Bush:

---

* www.janes.com, June 19, 2000.

† *Baltimore Sun*, February 8, 2001.

It's not clear the United States will ever need NMD to deal with emerging missile states; after all, there's no long-range threat yet, and if one emerges, there's no reason to believe that deterrence won't work.

Moreover, based on my analysis of the NMD, deploying that system would almost certainly be a net negative for U.S. security. It is likely to be ineffective against real attack, should one occur.

The real challenge in fielding an effective national defense is to be able to intercept real-world warheads, namely those that incorporate "countermeasures" designed to confuse or overwhelm the defense.

You should only consider deploying a system once tests have demonstrated that it can reliably intercept real-world targets using countermeasures. If you continue on the current path, even the first phase of the system would not be operational before at least 2007, and probably not before the end of your second term.

Move forward with deployment of a NMD system only if it is a net plus to overall U.S. security. You have to consider the reactions of other countries to NMD deployment, especially Russia and China. Perversely, NMD deployment will likely result in these countries responding by increasing their reliance on launch-on-warning.

Also, to the extent you are worried about emerging states, keep in mind that the United States needs Russian and Chinese co-operation to control missile and nuclear technology transfers to other countries.

Of course Bush and the Pentagon have completely ignored this advice and a great deal of other powerful evidence. On February 1, 2004, it was announced that the U.S. plans to have "a rudimentary missile defense system in operation by October." Moreover,

The Pentagon is seeking a 20 per cent boost in funding in 2005.

Yet,

The Missile Defense Agency plans only two full-fledged intercept tests before the system is declared operational.

Lisbeth Gronlund put it this way in an *American Prospect* on-line debate in 2001:

> For example, our report finds that an attacker could defeat the full NMD system by placing each nuclear warhead inside a mylar balloon to disguise it, and releasing it along with dozens of similar but empty balloons. Since none of the defense sensors would be able to determine which balloons contained warheads, the defense would have to shoot at all the balloons. But the attacker could deploy too many balloons for this to be possible.

Philip Coyle was the Assistant Secretary of Defense and Director of Operations and Test Evaluation at the Pentagon from 1994 to 2001. In an interview, he explains further:

> Out in space, a feather moves just as fast as a lead brick, and it's hard for us to think about that, but it does. So you can have a balloon that looks just like a re-entry vehicle floating along with a re-entry vehicle which is much heavier, much more dense, will have different aerodynamic properties when it finally gets close to the United States. But out in space, it's very hard to tell them apart.
>
> The problem with decoys and countermeasures is that your sensors, radar sensors on the ground and the infrared sensors on the interceptors, have to be able to tell these objects apart. They have to be able to tell the warhead . . . from all the other debris, things that are blinking and moving around, and which may look very similar to that re-entry vehicle.[*]

---

[*] Interview on *Frontline*, March 20, 2002. Lawrence Korb, former assistant secretary of defense in the Reagan administration, says Coyle now estimates that at least twenty more flight intercept tests and hundreds of subsystem tests will be required before the Pentagon would be ready for any realistic operational tests.

In the same debate, Stephen Young, then deputy director of the Coalition to Reduce Nuclear Dangers, said:

> The U.S. should not, under any circumstances, decide to deploy the proposed missile defense system. This system is a lemon and will never work effectively enough to make it worth the monetary and security costs it would entail.
>
> Why do I write this? Missile defense would seem to be a no-brainer. Who could oppose defending the United States against an attack by ballistic missiles? In fact, in the present situation, building a national missile defense would make the United States less secure, not more.
>
> This perhaps counterintuitive statement becomes apparent once one realizes that the current national missile defense proposal is architected for an unproven system that may never work and is designed against a threat that does not – and may never – exist. At the same time, deploying that defense may well undermine the entire non-proliferation regime, severely damaging relations with Russia and China – the only two potential U.S. adversaries that already have the ability to attack the United States with long-range missiles.

Young's arguments apply to Canada no less than to the United States: *the NMD will make Canada far less secure, not more.* But the rhetorical question he poses – how can anyone be against a missile defence shield? – lies behind the problem of public opinion polls on the subject. Walk down Robson Street, Jasper Avenue, Portage Avenue, Bloor Street, the Sparks Street Mall, Ste-Catherine Street, Barrington Street, or any place in Canada, and ask "Should we help the Americans build a missile shield that will prevent evil enemies from dropping nuclear bombs on your head, bombs that will totally destroy you and your family and everyone in your city?" Who would answer no to such a question?

But, ask "Should Canada participate in the NMD system when it's certain to drastically increase chances of a devastating nuclear war that could kill you and your family and destroy civilization?" and of course the answer will be entirely different.

Craig Eisendrath, Gerald Marsh, and Melvin Goodman are the authors of *The Phantom Defense: America's Pursuit of the Star Wars Illusion*, in which they systematically expose the technical deficiencies "that have plagued NMD for decades."* A summary of their research can be found at www.ciponline.org. The same authors have produced an excellent report in "Shield of Dreams: Why National Defense Won't Work." There's no room here to do justice to this first-class, fifteen-page analysis, but the following excerpts provide a very good historical background.

> On May 1, 2001, President Bush made his first presidential address on global issues, announcing that the United States "must move beyond the constraints of the thirty-year-old Anti-Ballistic Missile Treaty" and deploy an extensive and expensive shield against nuclear missiles. In doing so, the president withdrew the nation's support from principles that have governed the world's nuclear balance for the past three decades.

However,

> When analyzed carefully, it will be seen that none of the approaches to missile defense being considered works, or is likely to work, in the foreseeable future, and that deployment will lead to a new arms race, and will likely tear up the fabric of arms control agreements which have improved global security for over thirty years.
>
> National missile defense reflects an outmoded world view which fosters a unilateralist foreign policy.

The Center for International Policy report goes on to present a detailed and cogent analysis of "Why National Missile Defense Won't Work." It's

---

* *The Phantom Defense: America's Pursuit of the Star Wars Illusion*, Praeger, 2001.

difficult to read the analysis without concluding that Bush, Rumsfeld and colleagues are complete fools, or as is increasingly more certainly the case, that they have something very different in mind.

The (CIP) report goes on to discuss missile defence history and the international implications of Bush's NMD plans.

National missile defense was first proposed to counter a possible massive nuclear strike by the Soviet Union. A nuclear exchange with our principal Cold War rival, with its prospect of one hundred million deaths, was the nightmare scenario which haunted the first planners of an anti-ballistic-missile defense system as they began their work in the early 1960s.

The more scientists and technicians worked on such a system however, the less feasible it seemed. Prototype systems flunked test after test, or passed tests which so greatly simplified their task that success meant little or nothing. It would always be possible for the Soviets in a *real* situation to overwhelm the system by launching too many incoming missiles, and it would always be possible for the incoming missiles to avoid being hit by confusing the defending missiles with chaff and decoys. Finally, the cost of meeting an offensive challenge would always be many times higher than the cost of the offensive challenge itself.

After over a decade of research, both sides recognized the futility of going on with a missile defense system neither side could successfully develop. Pentagon planners also realized that the massive amount of dollars spent on a missile defense system which wouldn't work would drain money away from other systems which the military needed to guarantee U.S. security and protect our forces in the field.

Finally, the truth became inescapable. In 1972, President Richard Nixon and Soviet leader Leonid Brezhnev agreed to the Anti-Ballistic Missile (ABM) Treaty which forbade both sides from deploying a national missile-defense system, and restricted the testing which might make such a system possible. The treaty, which did allow the limited deployment of missile defenses, saw the United States install such a system in Grand Forks, North Dakota, at a cost of $6 billion, only to dismantle it immediately when it became clear it would be ineffective. The Soviets also deployed a limited missile defense system around Moscow, called *Galosh*, which the U.S. analysts also discounted as ineffective.

One of the arguments that led to Senate approval, with only two dissenting votes, of the ABM Treaty, in addition to the fact that anti-missile defense didn't work, was the fear that such a system would provoke the Soviet Union to stoke up the arms race, without increasing U.S. security. In other words, we would be worse off with the system than without it. A national missile-defense system was like a cap pistol; the other side thinking it was real, might shoot a real gun first.

Star Wars

Despite passage of the ABM Treaty, the Reagan administration took up the cause again in the 1980s, driven, in part, by the scientist Edward Teller's and the Livermore Laboratory's over-optimistic claims for a new, nuclear-bomb-driven X-ray laser. The rationale for a national missile-defense system was more political than strategic. As President Reagan knew, a generation of Americans had grown up under the shadow of a possible nuclear war. The doctrine of what had become known as Mutual Assured Destruction (MAD) could be seen as carrying a high moral price; if we could rely on defense, however, we could escape catastrophe without guilt. In addition, a strong nuclear-freeze movement put pressure on President Reagan to come up with an alternative to MAD. Once he proposed his Strategic Defense Initiative (SDI), or "Star Wars," his approval ratings shot up.

Ultimately, the Reagan administration spent tens of billions of dollars on the development of missile defense which the vast majority of scientists knew couldn't work, and which was banned by treaty. While President Reagan promised a "nuclear shield" that would achieve an "ultimate security" for the American people, such a system was never even conceivable. Nor was a system feasible which would be limited to protecting the ability of U.S. land-based missiles to survive and retaliate against a Soviet first strike. The initial emphasis of the X-ray laser was quietly dropped in 1984, when it became clear the concept was not viable, although the public was not told, and other options were explored, with equally dismal results. No system was ever found to be technically feasible, and no system was deployed. Periodic statements by the Union of Concerned Scientists and other scientific bodies made clear the opinion by the nation's scientists that SDI was not scientifically feasible, was a waste of money, and was a spur to the arms race.

The Bush Years After the Cold War

Although George Bush had disapproved of SDI as vice-president, in his 1988 presidential campaign he came out for full deployment and reinterpreting the ABM Treaty. High projected costs, however, led him to abandon the idea of a full NMD system, and to propose a limited system, renamed "Global Protection Against Accidental Launch System" (GPALS). Bush also called for the development of Theater Missile Defense programs against shorter-range missiles.

Waning appropriations were boosted by claims of success, advanced strenuously by then-Secretary of Defense Richard Cheney, of the U.S. Patriot missile during the Gulf War. These claims were later reduced by the General Accounting Office to state that Patriots hit only 9 per cent of the Scud warheads, and possibly none. Nevertheless, claims for the success of the Patriot have continued to fuel support for NMD.

Once again, a new anti-missile technology drove appropriations – autonomous, small kill vehicles lifted into outer space which would engage ICBMs. Called "Brilliant Pebbles," this system, like the X-ray laser, was advanced by Livermore Laboratory. Sky-rocketing costs – an estimated $85 billion – poor performance, and the clear threat the system posed to the ABM Treaty, including

strenuous Russian objections, doomed the system, and appropriations decreased. By the end of the Bush administration, over $100
billion had been spent on anti-missile research, making it the largest
weapons-research project in history and with virtually nothing to
show for it.

The Clinton Round

Following the 1994 "Contract with America" when the Republican
Congress attempted to mandate a national missile defense by 2003,
President Clinton vetoed the bill. In 1996 he sought to co-opt the
issue by devising a "Three Plus-Three" program, which supported
development of a national missile-defense system over three years,
and which designated 2000 as the year in which a decision would be
made whether to deploy the system over the *following* three years.
The system which could be deployed by 2003 would consist of
twenty ground-based interceptors, which if they worked, could
block missiles launched by "rogue states" or accidental launches by
Russia and China.

The option proposed by Clinton was a limited land-based
system designed to impact incoming missiles directly in outer
space. It was devised to counter a limited ballistic-missile strike by
a country like North Korea or Iran; it could not conceivably protect
the United States from a major ballistic-missile strike by Russia or
even from a significantly smaller strike by China. Estimates of the
system's cost ranged from $30 to 60 billion.

On September 1, 2000, President Clinton announced the decision to deploy a national missile-defense system would be left to the
next administration. Among the reasons cited were the system's
unproven technology, as dramatically brought home by a series of
failed tests; the unresolved possibility that countermeasures, such as
decoys, could foil it; and the objections of Russia, China, and our
NATO allies that deployment would jeopardize the 1972 ABM Treaty
and the texture of current arms-control agreements. Analysts also
pointed out that deployment could lead to a new arms race. If

China, for example, in response to NMD, greatly strengthened its force of ICBMs, India and possibly Japan would certainly respond, provoking a response from Pakistan.

Technical evaluation of the testing of national missile defense was complicated by the fact that testing often was conducted in situations considerably simpler than would be presented in reality. For instance, there would be an absence of decoys, or decoys with different reflecting surfaces from the warhead, or prior programmed information given to the anti-missile system of the flight characteristics of the warhead. Still another difficulty was created by the fact that the defense contractors who stood to gain by contracts were conducting the evaluations. Finally, the possibility of fraud and misrepresentation was raised by Dr. Nira Schwartz, a computer software expert at TRW, who maintained that the company had forced her to misrepresent her findings. These allegations are presently being investigated. Similar allegations of misrepresentation were made by Dr. Theodore Postol of MIT.

The Bush Round

As part of his campaign, and in the first few weeks of his administration, President George W. Bush called for early deployment of a national missile-defense system.

The systems under discussion include not only the mid-course, land-based system proposed by the Clinton administration, but also "boost-phase" systems, sea-based systems, expanded theater defenses, outer-space laser systems, and nuclear systems. Many of the same people and institutions involved in the earlier Reagan and Bush periods, including Secretary of Defense Rumsfeld; Frank Gaffney, who heads the Center for Security Policy; and Richard Perle, a foreign-policy adviser to President Bush; the Livermore Laboratory; the Heritage Foundation; corporations like Boeing, TRW, Raytheon, and Lockheed-Martin, are again working with members of Congress and contributing to their campaigns to push through national missile defense.

The ABM Treaty was based on the realistic proposition that offensive strategic forces could counter any innovations and rules out not just deployment but developmental testing for a national missile defense. It provides a useful impediment to the expansion of the arms race which national missile defense would induce.

Arms-control advocates and international lawyers consider the ABM Treaty the backbone of the arms-control regime and an obvious barrier to any current deployment of a national missile defense. The international community also shares this view. A unilateral reinterpretation of the treaty would undermine American credibility abroad and would violate the balance of powers established in the U.S. Senate. While the Reagan administration eventually accepted the restrictions on research of the treaty, the new Bush administration seems prepared to impose unilateral executive reinterpretation or abandon the treaty altogether. Its argument that the treaty is null and void because it was signed with the Soviet Union is specious, as Russia is clearly the legal inheritor of obligations undertaken by its predecessor.

But, of course, the Bush administration did exactly what was feared, and walked away from this "backbone of the arms-control regime," making the U.S. the first country to ever withdraw from a multilateral arms-control treaty.* The Center for International Policy report continues under the heading "American Unilateralism and National Missile Defense."

With the end of the Cold War, the United States emerged as the world's only superpower, a position we may well hold for some

---

* If ever there was a good example of the colonial mentality that has pervaded our foreign affairs bureaucrats, it was disgracefully evident when the U.S. announced its intentions to walk away from the ABM Treaty. Almost overnight, Canada's position changed from the treaty being a "vital cornerstone" of the efforts to curtail the dangers of nuclear war. Our response to the controversial U.S. action was muted, hesitant, and totally lacking in impact. In the words of one senior diplomat, "Nobody was too excited."

decades. What we choose to do with this power is up for question. The present administration believes it is our role to attempt to maintain and extend an encompassing world order which we define and which serves our national self-interest without constraint of international treaties or arrangements, including the current arms-control regime; if we do so, it believes the world will benefit. It is no accident that those who support NMD also opposed the Anti-Ballistic Missile Treaty, the Strategic Arms Reduction Talks (START) treaties, the Outer Space Treaty, the Comprehensive Nuclear Test Ban, and the International Criminal Court.[*] For them, arms control represents a "Cold War mentality."

If the decision is made to go ahead with NMD it will likely involve the alienation of Russia and China from the arms-control process; and the end of American leadership to stop proliferation of nuclear weapons. National missile defense would destabilize American national security policy and greatly increase American defense spending. It would register a net decrease in U.S. security, exchanging an inadequate defense for the abrogation of two important treaties and the ensuing instability.

Alternatives to NMD

Instead of national missile defense, the United States should be looking for ways to reduce nuclear inventories in this country and abroad. The United States should work closely with Russia to support co-operative efforts to secure Russian nuclear materials and weapons, a policy which is presently under threat should funds be reduced.

The United States should also abandon its launch-on-warning doctrine and its doctrine that we would be the first to employ

---

[*] The International Criminal Court, created to hear cases involving war crimes, is headed by a Canadian, Judge Philippe Kirsch. George W. Bush explained that the U.S. would not support the court because he feared that American soldiers would be hauled into the court, which would be "very troubling." It's difficult not to consider this in relation to the appalling behaviour of more than a few U.S. troops in Iraq.

nuclear weapons under certain circumstances. A no-first-use pledge that included the United States, Russia, and China (already given), and perhaps Britain and France, would make it easier to impose sanctions against any state that was a base for nuclear terrorists or that planned to use nuclear weapons.

The Alternative to Unilateralism

The larger geopolitical issue is whether the United States will continue to follow a policy of unilateralism or pursue a policy of multilateralism. U.S. support for multilateralism in the diplomatic arena would enable Washington to establish the machinery and rules for international peacekeeping, counter-proliferation, and avoidance of regional conflict. A more stable international system should be the goal. National missile defense, which would deny this option, is not in the national interest.

But, of course, Bush, Rumsfeld et al. ignored all of this advice. John Isaacs, president of the Council for a Livable World in Washington, D.C., accuses the Bush administration of deploying a system that is "deaf, dumb and blind."

> The planned deployment lacks a needed radar system to make it see, operational tests to determine if it works and satellite systems to provide adequate sensors."

In December 2003, the respected Washington, D.C., Center for Arms Control and Non-Proliferation said that a thorough analysis on the NMD plans "fails on practically all counts." For example, how plausible is an attack by North Korea?

> It would be an act of lunacy for the Koreans to launch a missile attack against us, knowing the kind of retaliation that would inevitably follow.

Just as it's unlikely that the NMD system could actually destroy an ICBM, the chances of an attack by Kim Jong-il "is minuscule." Would the NMD be effective against terrorists? Of course not.

What about al-Qaeda or some other terrorist group? Terrorists would surely not be deterred by any threat of retaliation; they have repeatedly demonstrated their readiness to commit suicide in pursuit of their objectives. But, even if a terrorist group managed to steal a nuclear weapon, it is most unlikely to gain access to intercontinental missiles as well as the means to launch and guide them.

Then we return to the question of whether or not the system will actually work.

All tests to date have been carried out under unrealistic conditions. For example, the defense has been told the launch points and launch time. No comprehensive tests have been carried out on missiles launched without advance notice and equipped with sophisticated decoys. No tests have been carried out at night or against multi targets. In two embarrassing failures, the kill vehicle failed to separate from the booster.

Moreover, the two new advanced satellite systems required for NMD have not been designed and no

configuration has yet been decided, and no operational testing is likely this decade. Never has so inadequately tested a weapons system been deployed by the U.S. military.

At the present rate of testing it could take ten years or more before the effectiveness of the system is demonstrated.

Meanwhile, tests have been cancelled, and "others have been dumbed down to less demanding tasks."

Why the rush? A cynic might point out that the scheduled deployment date is just a month before the 2004 election. The president will announce with great fanfare that for the first time, American cities are protected from attack by enemy missiles. And the public will be unaware of what a sham that protection will be.[*]

In July 2003 the forty-thousand-member American Physical Society representing U.S. physicists issued a study showing that the NMD plans would not be an effective approach for defending the U.S. against boost-phase missiles from countries such as North Korea or Iran:

> Only two or three minutes would be available to achieve a boost-phase intercept, even assuming substantial improvements in systems for detecting and tracking missiles. . . . In the most optimistic scenarios, the defense would have only seconds to decide whether to fire interceptors and could be required to make this decision before knowing whether a rocket launch was a space mission or a missile attack.

The study was conducted by a group that included recognized experts on missile defence.

> A system of space-based interceptors . . . would require a fleet of a thousand or more orbiting satellites just to intercept a single missile.

And, for all Canadians,

> Although a successful intercept would prevent munitions from reaching their target, live nuclear, biological, or chemical warheads could strike populated areas short of the target in the United States or in other countries. This "shortfall problem" is inherent in any boost-phase defense and difficult to avoid.

---

[*] Leo Sartori, Center for Arms Control and Non-Proliferation, December 3, 2003.

And why the rush in Canada? In a January 2004 letter to Paul Martin, Ernie Regehr, points out that

> One year ago, the Standing Committee on Foreign Affairs and International Trade advised the Government not to make any decision on BMD because "the technology, has not been proven and details of deployment are not known." Events since then only reinforce the wisdom of that caution.
> During 2003, four U.S. General Accounting Office investigations confirmed that none of 10 essential technologies has been tested in operational conditions and 8 of 10 have not even reached the product development stage.

Moreover,

> The proposed system will not provide any protection to Canadians – neither when it is constructed in 2004 and 2005, nor in the foreseeable future.

The Union of Concerned Scientists says this:

> The system the Bush administration plans to deploy by 2004 will have essentially no defense capability. The technology needed for an effective missile-defense system still doesn't exist. By 2004–2006 operational testing will not have begun and test conditions will remain far from realistic.*

So, what happens to the NMD system if the Russians or the Chinese or the Koreans, or who have you, as would be certain, employ multiple independently targeted re-entry vehicles (MIRVs) and a great number of decoys on their missiles? What happens is easy to predict. Any missile

---

* www.ucsusa.org

defence system, even if an effective one ever becomes operational many years and many hundreds of billions of dollars down the road, will be easily overwhelmed and hence will be largely ineffective.

Now, let's turn to our own Department of National Defence's previously secret report referred to earlier. Here we learn that:

- the planned missile defence shield would be useless against low-flying cruise missiles or unmanned drones fitted with WMD [weapons of mass destruction].
- The shield would result in "competitor states" that would seek to "overwhelm missile defences through qualitative and quantitative improvements" in their fleets of missiles or other delivery vehicles.
- "If you were positioned off Halifax and fired one of these, you could take out that port quite nicely, because there are no defences employed that could knock down a cruise missile."
- "Such a scenario would give the U.S. or Canada little warning of an attack."
- "Ballistic missile defence is designed to deal with ballistic missiles."

Supposing only one single missile, no matter how delivered, got through the NMD system. It would likely have multiple warheads with a five hundred kiloton yield at least thirty-five times more powerful than the bomb that destroyed Hiroshima. If a single missile hit Toronto, it would likely kill over a million people, it would decimate almost everything between Bloor and the waterfront, and between Broadview and Jane. The entire area would be uninhabitable for decades; the effects of radiation would continue to impact the population for at least twenty years, and probably much longer.

Ghastly and virtually unimaginable as this would be, it is still most likely a quite conservative estimate of the horrific results. Dom Stasi, an American engineer and pilot who has been a member of the Project Apollo technical team and has worked with missile defence contractors in engineering flight and systems ground testing, has written a brilliant essay about how hopelessly ineffective the NMD system will be and what the consequences will be.

At altitude now, the offensive missile deploys its multiple warheads and more multiple decoys. Each warhead an ablative shell designed to withstand the fires of reentry. Each vehicle potentially housing and protecting a multi-megaton yield atomic bomb, they all begin their long fall back to planet Earth. Each follows a separate and confusing path. Three follow an indistinct but guided trajectory. In all they form a macabre ensemble swan dive toward the familiar land mass below: the United States. Minutes later, and completely without effective warning to their people, the cities of New York, Boston, and Washington, D.C., are vaporized by a searing white heated shockwave. Expanding at 20,000 feet per second in all directions, the white-hot hurricanes destroy everything in three separate twenty-mile radii. Millions die instantly.

Communications-, civil-, and disaster-relief infrastructures are spared none of the weapon's fury. As the three mushroom clouds rise into the stratosphere, all is silent beneath their convergent plumes. There are no sirens. No rescuers. There is no way into the devastated cities, no way out, and no hope of either recovery or rational retaliation. Over the ensuing days, those millions not mercifully vaporized by the impossible blast will endure the unimaginable agonies of radiation poisoning, incineration's aftermath, and ultimately agonizing and tortuous decline into a welcomed stupor of trauma, starvation, and shock. There will be no anesthetic, only agony. There will be no rescuers, only a beseeched – and for those fortunate enough to succumb – a merciless death.

But as horrible as the aforementioned might be to contemplate, more horrible still is the realization that what I've described is what could happen if the United States were so attacked AFTER it bought and finally deployed the costly and ultimately useless missile-defense system Mr. Bush is proposing. What our president does not want you to know is this: as currently anticipated, the missile defense system he is endorsing and funding with your children's money will greatly enrich his private defense contractor cronies (the usual suspects), but it will protect the United States and her people from nothing. Nothing. Nothing!*

In February 2004, CBC News correspondent Lisa Schlein from Geneva reported that

A Senior United Nations official says millions of victims of Chernobyl, the world's biggest peacetime nuclear disaster, remain forgotten and neglected. Radiation from the Chernobyl nuclear reactor in Ukraine, which exploded in April 1986, contaminated vast areas of Byelorusse, Ukraine and Russia.

The United Nations estimates more than seven million people still are suffering from the effects of Chernobyl nearly 18 years after the nuclear power accident occurred. It notes 23 per cent of Byelorusse, the hardest hit area, is contaminated from the radiation emitted by the plant and will remain so for hundreds of years to come. UN Under-Secretary-General for Humanitarian Affairs, Jan Egeland has just returned from the region. He says about 200 villages have been abandoned at a cost of 235 billion U.S. dollars.

Egeland says radiation poisoning has caused a large increase in thyroid cancer among children and long-term genetic effects.

For John Polanyi:

One does not need to be a rocket scientist to see that this program is headed for embarrassment and subsequent oblivion. It won't work, so why do we play along with the U.S.?†

---

* www.spectacle.org. Stasi's entire article is well worth reading.

† www.commissiononglobalization.org, October 2003.

Ernie Regehr restates another point:

> An attacking missile would not necessarily be destroyed but would simply be knocked off course and would continue roughly along its original trajectory, but would fall short of its intended target – with obvious implications for Canada in the case of missiles targeted on the United States and on a flight trajectory over Canadian territory.*

Will the system work? Here's testimony of scientists from the Massachusetts Institute of Technology, and the Union of Concerned Scientists, as quoted in Ernie Regehr's report:

> The system the United States will deploy in September 2004 will have essentially *no* defense capability. Even if the technology worked perfectly, countermeasures are easy to build . . .

Regehr continues:

> Even when it matures, strategic missile defence is not intended, nor will it ever have the capacity, to protect Americans or Canadians from the primary arsenal of missiles capable of striking North America.

Referring to countermeasures against BMD, *The Economist*† says

> Some skeptics claim countermeasures would render the whole enterprise useless. Critics allege that politics, not science, is behind what they label "a rush to failure."

---

* There has been some speculation that a successful intercept of a missile over Canada would result in a "Chernobyl-like" distribution of radioactive material over thousands of square kilometres on Canadian territory.

† December 6, 2003.

In an excellent article in the *National Security Studies Quarterly*,* Dr. John Steinbruner, director for the Center for International Security Studies and professor of public policy at the University of Maryland, makes some valuable points:

> The best that can plausibly be claimed for the national missile defense scheme . . . is it would provide unreliable protection against an improbable form of threat. . . . The entire project promises to stimulate threats it cannot handle.
>
> Therein lies the reason it is considered to be so provocative. No one is prepared to believe the United States – or more precisely, its decision makers – is now or would forever remain that stupid. Potential strategic opponents are compelled to assume the nonsensically limited system is but a stalking horse for a more serious effort . . . the further elaboration of the already imposing offensive capabilities of U.S. forces.
>
> Against an initiating opponent who can choose the timing and operational details of an attack, the proposed U.S. system is basically worthless.
>
> When viewed from the perspective of a potential opponent, the NMD program appears to be an effort to establish a degree of superiority sufficient to eliminate any threat – that is any opposing deterrent capacity.
>
> That, of course, is an alarming prospect to the two major societies, Russia and China, who consider themselves to be potential opponents and are committed to preserving a credible deterrent capability. In principle, Russia's deterrent force is based on thousands of nuclear weapons, more than enough to overwhelm a U.S. defensive system.
>
> Both Russia and China have reasons for concern that the eroding credibility of their deterrent capacity would expose them to

---

* *National Security Studies Quarterly*, vol. VI, issue 3, summer 2000.

serious intimidation from the ever more capable and intrusive U.S. conventional forces.... Each in their own way can be expected to resist such an outcome with every means at their disposal [including] an expansion and technical elaboration of offensive weapons deployments in order to assure survival and penetration of the missile shield.

Reader, I hope you will have noted carefully the second paragraph of John Steinbruner's comments above. It is in fact, to a very large degree, what this book is all about. John Polanyi puts it this way:

The NMD program will cost at least $1 trillion.

At best, it would be only partially effective. As U.S. Senator Joe Biden, former chair of the U.S. foreign relations committee, said sarcastically, "How splendid the NMD would give our leaders the option of only losing San Francisco or Chicago."

Other nations, China, Pakistan, India will feel obligated to follow the NMD path. Unchecked, weapons and counterweapons lead only to the development of further weapons.

Three years ago, *The Economist* put it succinctly:

What folly for Americans to spend billions on missile defences, while unraveling the rules which limit the weapons that may someday get through or around them.[*]

Okay then, if there is a long-standing and growing and overwhelming consensus that the American NMD plan is *not* going to work, surely then there are two important questions that Canadians must ask. First, *why* is the U.S. government plunging ahead with their plans? And second, *why* in God's name are Paul Martin, Bill Graham, and the rest of the Canadian government planning to join in?

---

[*] *The Economist*, September 8, 2001.

As I have already implied, and as we shall see in the next chapter, there are some obvious answers to the first question. There are absolutely *no logical answers* to the second question.

A few more words here about North Korea. In an article for the Council for a Livable World, under the heading "Missile Defense: The Dangers and Lack of Realism," George Rathjens, a former Chief Scientist with the U.S. Department of Defense, and Carl Kaysen, who was Deputy Special Assistant to John F. Kennedy for national security affairs, write

> there is not now even the remotest prospect that a near-term defense of population against a determined attack by a major power (Russia or China) would be effective.

But, what about North Korea?

> We question Secretary of Defense Rumsfeld's statements that North Korea (or perhaps another aspirant nuclear weapons state) would deliver a nuclear first strike once it had a capacity to do so.
>
> It is more reasonable to assume that North Korea's rationale for acquiring a nuclear ICBM capacity has been similar to that of the United States, to be able to deter another nation with strong military capabilities (in North Korea's case, the United States; in that of the United States, the Soviet Union) from involvement in regions of conflict inimical to its interests.

The Center for Arms Control and Non-Proliferation has this to say about North Korea and the NMD plans:

> The stated mission is to defend the United States from a missile attack launched by some rogue state, initially North Korea. How plausible is such an attack? North Korea is pursuing a nuclear weapons program, and has tested some intermediate-range ballistic

missiles. In time, it might have a few missiles capable of reaching the United States, and might be able to arm them with nuclear warheads. But it would be an act of lunacy for the Koreans to launch a missile attack against us, knowing the kind of retaliation that would inevitably follow.

During the Cold War the Soviet Union, with a far greater offensive capability than North Korea ever can hope to achieve, was deterred from using nuclear weapons against us. Unless Kim Jong-il has suicidal tendencies, he has no intention of using his nuclear capability, if he ever attains one, in a ballistic missile strike against the United States.

There is another possible mission not prominently discussed by the administration. Possession of a nuclear capacity, even a tiny one, would give North Korea some degree of deterrence against us. If President Bush (or some future president) were to contemplate attacking N. Korea, he might be dissuaded from doing so if he feared that the Koreans could deliver even one or two nuclear-armed missiles on American soil. This is in fact the most plausible motive for N. Korea to pursue a nuclear program.[*]

This chapter has already become too long. But, should you want a quick history of the decades of failure of American missile-defence aspirations, go to Fred Kaplan's excellent December 17, 2002 *Slate* article, "Bush's indefensible missile-defense plan." Some brief excerpts:

No matter how good defenses might get, any "rogue" with enough sophistication to build and launch a ballistic missile can easily maneuver around those defenses. On this last point, it is worth noting that U.S. weapons scientists and intelligence analysts have known about these maneuvering tricks for more than 40 years; that no one has the slightest idea of how to deal with them; and that Bush's current test program does not even attempt to do so. . . .

---

[*] Leo Sartori, October 2003.

During the Cold War, holding each other's population hostage – the essence of MAD – was seen as the way to deter either the United States or the U.S.S.R. from launching a nuclear first-strike. Mounting a defense against nuclear strikes, some argued, might erode deterrence. The Anti-Ballistic Missile Treaty of 1972, which sharply limited (and, in later revisions, banned) missile defenses, is viewed in this light as the apotheosis of MAD. . . .

The United States (and the U.S.S.R.) gave up on nuclear defenses – not just ABMs, but also nationwide fallout shelters – not out of obeisance to deterrence theory, but because the calculations were clear that offense would always beat defense. And because the technology seemed out of reach, the effort seemed fruitless, in any case. That's why Richard Nixon and Leonid Brezhnev – neither arms-control softies – signed the ABM Treaty.

The treaty reflected an acceptance of analysis conducted over the previous 15 years, not by doves but by Pentagon engineers and White House physicists, many of them hawks who despaired over their findings. . . .

In 1961, Kennedy's defense secretary, Robert McNamara, ordered his own study, with similar results. The prospect of a "really effective" missile-defense system, the 55-page report concluded, "is bleak, has always been so, and there are no great grounds for hope that the situation will markedly improve in the future, no matter how hard we try." The main reason: "No one has yet suggested any solution to the problem of overcoming very simple, lightweight, non-discriminable decoys."*

Jump ahead to the latest chapter of this apparently never-ending saga. In September 1999, the CIA's National Intelligence Estimate concluded that any country able to develop ballistic missiles "would also develop various responses to U.S. defenses,"

---

* Readers who haven't seen the recent film about Robert McNamara, *The Fog of War*, should make every effort to do so.

including such "readily available technology" as decoys, chaff, or wrapping warheads in radar-absorbing material. . . .

When Deputy Defense Secretary Paul Wolfowitz said in an Oct. 24 speech that we are "moving forward on missile defenses" to the point where "we actually can hit a bullet with a bullet," he was uttering an irrelevancy. Hitting one bullet with one bullet is certainly a remarkable feat, but it's among the least remarkable feats that an effective missile-defense system must accomplish.

Incidentally, no tests have yet involved hitting, say, two bullets with two bullets. . . .

In a lengthy analysis in December 2003, the Center for Arms Control and Non-Proliferation examines the mission of the NMD system, questions how much it will contribute to U.S. security, asks if it will work and whether it is cost-effective, and wonders if it will have any unintended consequences that adversely affect U.S. security? The conclusion is succinctly stated: "as currently configured it fails on practically all counts."

But all this said, let's really stretch things, and stretch them very far, and let's just suppose that somehow, years into the future, the U.S. system will be able to shoot down as many as half of all the incoming ICBMs from Russia, or China, or where have you. That would still certainly mean the destruction of pretty well every city in the U.S., and in Canada too, if we join in the NMD system. To imagine a perfect success rate against manoeuvrable missiles with decoys is absurd. To imagine even a 25 per cent success rate defies all logic.

Everyone who is the slightest bit interested in the topic knows that later this year the U.S. will begin deploying a hugely expensive system with zero evidence that it will work. You would think, at the very least, there would be an accelerated schedule of tests to assess and attempt to improve its effectiveness. Instead, in March 2003 we learned that most flight tests scheduled for 2003 and 2004 have been either cancelled or delayed to 2005. And the first-ever flight test of an actual interceptor with a small "kill vehicle" was not scheduled until a few weeks before operational deployment. The test, which will likely be publicized, is considered to be a "fly-by," i.e., the interceptor is not required to hit the target.*

On March 12, 2004, James Glanz of the *New York Times* reported that

> ... project officials faced intense questioning at a Senate Armed Services Committee hearing on Thursday. . . .
>
> Senator Jack Reed of Rhode Island said "Standing up there and saying, this is a deployed system that will protect this country against a real threat stretches my imagination."
>
> . . . Some critics say they see only one thing on the horizon that could be driving the project's breakneck schedule: a presidential election season. . . .
>
> The hearing came as the General Accounting Office released a report that contained criticisms of the program. The office said that . . . none of the components of the system had been tested in "its deployed configuration."
>
> Senator Carl Levin . . . asked General Kadish [director of the Missile Defense Agency at the Pentagon], "Is there any relationship between [the president's decision to deploy the system], and that shortly thereafter you decided to cancel all these tests?"
>
> In an interview, the former director of the Pentagon's operational test and evaluation office Philip E. Coyle said "Ever since the president made his decision, the priority . . . has been on deployment, not on understanding whether the system works. Most people don't appreciate how complicated this system is, nor how much all of the tests so far have been artificially scripted to be successful."

---

* Thomas Christie, director of the Pentagon's Office of Operational Test and Evaluation, says "Even with successful intercepts . . . the small number of tests would limit confidence."

What follows is from Senator Carl Levin's opening statement to the Armed Services Committee hearing on March 11, 2004

The administration's . . . budget request for missile defense is truly staggering . . . the largest single-year funding request for any weapon system in history.

The majority of this funding is in pursuit of a rudimentary and uncertain defense against an unlikely long-range missile attack.

To put the missile defense budget request in perspective, this request is close to twice the entire budget request for U.S. Customs and Border Protection in the Department of Homeland Security, a program dedicated to keep would-be terrorists out of our country. The missile defense request is more than double the next largest annual request for a weapon system, the F-22 fighter jet, and is more than the entire annual research and development budget of the United States Army. . . .

If we spend this money, will we actually get an effective defense for this country – or will we get instead a system that was rushed to the field prematurely, that will have to be fixed, and fixed again at enormous additional costs as operational tests reveal significant problems? . . .

The administration plans to deploy a National Missile Defense system in September – which is just six short months away. This is despite the fact that the last major test of the system was more than one year ago, and was a failure.

Then inexplicably, seven of the eight intercept tests of the system that had been scheduled for 2003 and 2004 have either been cancelled or have been delayed until next year.

The plan to deploy in September remains, despite the fact that only one of the intercept tests which were to occur before deployment is still planned. Even that test will be a well-scripted event in which the system's radar will not be functioning. Instead, the target itself will broadcast its position to the missile defense system.

A real enemy missile heading towards the United States will not be broadcasting its position to us. . . . And the system the administration plans to deploy in September will have completed no realistic tests. Zero.

Both the U.S. Office of Management and Budget, and Congress's General Accounting Office raised serious concerns about the missile defence plans, especially the lack of adequate preparedness and the burgeoning cost overruns. Moreover, there is growing skepticism that future goals can be met. A major criticism is the lack of cost projections for developing and operating the system, termed "a major flaw" causing "friction" within the Pentagon.

Meanwhile the Missile Defense Agency admitted that key elements of the system would not be ready in time for the scheduled deployment. As a result, "the agency so far has had to put navigational transmitters on targets to track them during its intercept tests." Jim Stoffels sums it all up nicely:

What will we be deploying? After 20 years of development and some $100 billion of taxpayer money, the hardware produced by the Missile Defense Agency and its predecessors has not approached the functionality of a Model T. . . .

Trying to make a NMD system work is itself an exercise in futility. Like the Maginot Line, even a working system could easily be circumvented by much less complex technology. . . .

Given that the history of the program is fraught with failure, fraud and coverup, it is difficult to credit the true believers with protecting anything more than the profits of the weapons industry.*

Indeed, a valid explanation. But, for the *real* impetus behind the White House and Pentagon plans, see the next chapter.

---

* www.wcpeace.org/bmd.htm

Meanwhile, in both the U.S. and Canada, the military and the bureaucrats have been misleading the politicians and the public. Here are excerpts from the testimony of Lt. General Ronald Kadish, soon-to-be-replaced director of the Pentagon's Missile Defense Agency, to the U.S. Senate Armed Services Committee, March 11, 2004:

> ... the system can be very effective against countermeasures.
> ... most of the well-publicized flight tests have been successful.
> ... Wherever possible we are making every test both operationally realistic and developmental.
> ... ballistic missile defense has proven itself technologically possible.

James R. Wright is Assistant Deputy Minister, Global and Security Policy, Department of Foreign Affairs and International Trade. He appeared before the Canadian Senate's Standing Committee on National Security and Defence on February 23, 2004, and three days later before the House of Commons Standing Committee on National Defence and Veterans Affairs. Some excerpts from Wright:

> ... Ballistic missile defence will be an operational reality in the U.S. in the very near future.
> ... BMD would complement, not compete with, Canada's non-proliferation, arms control and disarmament efforts.
> ... I know the U.S. government has worked very hard with our Russian and Chinese colleagues to ensure that those countries, those governments, have a proper appreciation of exactly what it is that the United States has in mind here.
> ... The ballistic missile defence program has had, I believe, eight tests, five of which have been successful. I think we can assume that our U.S. colleagues will be striving to improve the quality of the marksmanship to bring it up to 100 per cent.
> ... All you need do is read the editorials and the op-ed pieces in newspapers across the country to recognize that for most Canadians, this makes perfectly good sense.

. . . Our two countries share unprecedented levels of interoperability, coupled with a common objective of fostering both continental security and greater international peace and security.

. . . We are working to see whether . . . we can breathe some life into the arms control and disarmament debates.

. . . I don't think anyone today would agree that ballistic missile defence constitutes an offensive system.

. . . Re multilateral arms control and disarmament in all international fora . . . our credentials remain impeccable.

. . . Russia does not see missile defence representing a strategic threat against Russia.

One could easily fill a volume criticizing Wright's contentious statements before these committees. Yet he is the one who has been "leading the discussions on Canadian participation in the program with the U.S."

I want to get on to the next chapter, one of the most important in the book. But, before I do, I have one other observation about Wright's testimony. The quality of the questions that the senators posed for the witness was appallingly weak. And, with only a few exceptions from Bloc, NDP, and a few Liberal Members of Parliament, the MPs were no better.

Lastly, I have to return to our former defence minister, David Pratt, who appeared before the House of Commons Standing Committee of National Defence and Veterans Affairs on April Fool's Day, 2004. Following are some of his comments:

Mr. Chairman, my information coming from the Department of National Defence, which had some fairly close contact with the U.S. Department of Defense, is that five of the last eight tests have been successful. The level of sophistication of these tests has increased significantly over the last two years to the point where, in fact, the tests have involved decoys where a missile is fired. The interceptor goes up to hit it and there are decoys that are used to try, in effect, to fool the missile. Even under those conditions there has been success. Even the last test, I believe, was quite successful.

What nonsense. Either Pratt was somehow very poorly briefed, or he was misleading the committee. Or perhaps it's both. I asked Dr. Lisbeth Gronlund, who is now Co-Director and Senior Scientist, Global Security Program, Union of Concerned Scientists, to comment on Pratt's testimony. On the telephone from Boston she said she was "stunned" by Pratt's "blatant inaccuracies." I asked her to comment further in writing:

> The interceptor advance has been provided with a detailed set of a priori information about the trajectory and appearance of the objects that are to be targets, including the warheads and the decoys, plus detailed information about flight plans and characteristics. The interceptor is provided with information re the exact position of the mock warhead using a GPS receiver or a C-band beacon located on the warhead. Flight tests planned through to the fall of 2007 "are not designed to address the challenge of countermeasures that have been identified as simple for an enemy to implement. The tests have not demonstrated realistic engagement conditions and have essentially been repeats of previous tests with identical engagement conditions: same time of day, same weather conditions, same intercept geometry, same fly-out range, same altitude of intercept, etc.

And, by the way, the last test Pratt referred to did not result in an intercept. The kill vehicle interceptor and booster rocket failed to even separate. Nine tests have been put off or cancelled since then. Chuck Spinney, who was a U.S. Defense Department program analyst says, "It's not testing . . . They've [sic] just been demonstrations. Star Wars can never work . . . It's just a boondoggle."*

As for Pratt's colleague, Liberal Senate Defence Committee Chairman Colin Kenny, he says, "What's so sacred about weapons in space?"

In late April 2004, Congress's General Accounting Office presented its fourth highly critical review of the Pentagon's plans, including

---

* John Isaacs, Council for a Livable World, June 28, 2004, www.clw.org.

complaints about incomplete information, repeated delays, escalating costs, absence of traditional oversight requirements, failure to specify ongoing operational costs, etc. But, yet again, the focus was on the rigged testing:

> Critics also note that the tests so far have all been tightly choreo-graphed. The pace is slower than a real engagement. . . . A global positioning system aboard the target guides the interceptor. And the sensors are told in advance how to identify the warhead. "It only works if you assume that the other side plays along," says Richard Garwin, a physicist and weapons expert who was a member of the Rumsfeld commission.[*]

Noted physicist Theodore Postol believes a mid-course defence system is certain to fail. "I can guarantee it won't work." Simply enclosing the warhead in an aluminum-coated mylar balloon and releasing similar balloons as decoys would be enough to befuddle the most sophisticated radar and sensors. In Philip Coyle's words: "If they're smart enough to build ICBMs, they're smart enough to build countermeasures."[†]

Though not admitting it publicly, Pentagon officials understand this. Hence the concentration on boost-phase missiles and weapons in space. The forty-thousand-member American Physical Society con-cluded that "none of the boost-phase defense concepts studied would be viable for the foreseeable future."

Among the many detailed points their study makes is this:

> An ICBM which did not have its munition incapacitated by an inter-ceptor hit would continue on a ballistic trajectory and impact earth short of the target. For both North Korea and Iran, the likely area of impact includes Canada. This risk is inherent to boost-phase missile defense.

---

[*] John Isaacs, www.clw.org, April 26, 2004.
[†] Ibid.

A month later, thirty-one former Washington officials sent a strong letter to President Bush saying that the planned missile defence system "will provide no real defense" and calling it a "sham." The officials had worked at the Pentagon, Department of State, National Security Council, the Arms Control and Disarmament Agency, and other government offices, and for presidents Eisenhower, Kennedy, Johnson, Nixon, Carter, Reagan, George H.W. Bush, and Clinton.[*]

Richard Garwin, who advised many U.S. governments on security, describes the current NMD plans as "totally useless" and says that George W. Bush is "wasting money and he's impairing our security because it will not work against ICBMs from anyone who has it in for the United States."

Only a few days later, the Union of Concerned Scientists produced a lengthy and scathing report saying that the Bush missile defence system:

> will have no demonstrated defensive capability and will be ineffective against a real attack by long-range missiles . . . no realistic testing has been held . . . the system will be vulnerable to even simple countermeasures. . . . The administration's claims that the system will be reliable and highly effective are irresponsible exaggerations.[†]

Contrast all of this with the testimony to our Commons and Senate Defence Committees by David Pratt and James Wright.

---

[*] John Isaacs, www.clw.org, May 7, 2004.

[†] www.ucsusa.org

"A Nuclear Arsenal in Space":
Approving What We Have Always Opposed

————————————————

It is not credible for Canada to seek involvement and claim that
such involvement does not imply support for the space-based ele-
ments that it knows Washington is actively pursuing.
    – Ernie Regehr in *Canadian Ballistic Missile Defence*

Let me begin this chapter with the most recent words available at the time of writing from our foreign affairs minister and our former defence minister, about the weaponizing of space. Here's Bill Graham, this time in the House of Commons, just prior to the vote on the February 2004 Bloc motion asking that Canada withdraw from NMD talks with the U.S.:

In our view, it does not lead to an arms race, nor does it lead to the weaponization of space.

Earlier, Graham again promised that Canada would pull out of any NMD negotiations with the U.S., if it were shown that the Pentagon wanted to deploy weapons in space.[*] Keep that in mind as you go through the rest of this chapter.

Now let's hear from David Pratt:

————

[*] *National Post*, February 25, 2004.

The U.S. policy on missile defence has absolutely nothing to do with the weaponization of space.

I would simply say that what we are looking at is a limited system of land and sea based interceptors.*

So, remember, the NMD plans have "absolutely nothing to do with the weaponization of space."

It's worth reading the following sentence from the Union of Concerned Scientists again:

The system the Bush administration plans to deploy by 2004 will have essentially no defense capability.

Obviously then, the question must follow, *why* are the Americans building the NMD, knowing full well that it won't work, and that it is already having a dangerously destabilizing effect on world security?

According to former prime minister Jean Chrétien, Canada remains firmly opposed to the weaponizing of space. In May 2003 Chrétien said

There will not be a program in which we will participate if it means the weaponizing of space.

Foreign Affairs Minister Bill Graham has said that "Canada's clear policy is that we are against the weaponizing of space." And also that "Space-based weapons are immoral, illegal, and a bad mistake." Got that? Immoral, illegal, and a bad mistake.

But, while Jean Chrétien was saying that Ottawa would pull out of talks if the U.S plans to weaponize space, his own minister of defence, John McCallum, and his chief of defence staff, both fully aware of the NMD program's implications for space, were down in Washington "investigating," if not yet formally planning the details of Canada's participation.

---

* House of Commons, February 23, 2004.

It's too bad that Paul Martin, Bill Graham, David Pratt, John McCallum, and Stephen Harper somehow haven't been able to find the time to read the Pentagon document entitled "Rebuilding America's Defenses." It says it all very clearly:

> Unrestricted use of space has become a major strategic interest of the United States. . . . [We must have] freedom of operation within space and an ability to deny others the use of space.

Once again, it can't be much clearer than that, can it?

In contrast to John Ibbitson, *Globe and Mail* columnist Jeffrey Simpson has written one of the very best columns on the American plans:

> Just as the conquest of Iraq was not fundamentally about weapons of mass destruction, so the U.S. anti-ballistic missile system is not about protecting the United States from missiles. It's about placing weapons in space.
>
> If Canada joins the U.S. system – it will be approving what it has always opposed.
>
> The U.S. has already militarized space. Satellites are an indispensable part of the U.S. military machine. It will not be long before the U.S. moves to place weapons in space, a policy proposed by Defense Secretary Donald Rumsfeld before he entered the Bush administration.
>
> Anti-missile defence without weaponizing space is like being half-pregnant. Joining the missile defence scheme without understanding where it must lead is to misunderstand the stakes.
>
> The salesmanship for anti-missile defence is almost entirely specious. Under what conceivable ground would "rogue states" have the motivation [to attack the U.S.] knowing that the destruction of their countries beckoned?*

---

* *Globe and Mail*, May 7, 2003.

Or, as someone in Great Britain put it

> Any state stupid enough to throw anything bigger than a grenade at
> the U.S. would be bombed back into the Stone Age.*

Let's go back to Donald Rumsfeld, the developed world's most
aggressive warlord. Prior to becoming Defense Secretary, Rumsfeld was
the chairman of the U.S. Commission to Assess National Security
Space Management and Organization. The commission recommended
the creation of a U.S. Space Corps with military capability. By deploying surveillance and weapons, the U.S. would be able to "control space"
and "dominate" the world.

Subsequently, the U.S. Air Force has produced a detailed plan "to
fight from and in space," to provide "our vision of controlling and fully
exploiting space . . . . To dominate the globe, the United States must
dominate outer space."

The U.S. plans clearly violate the 1967 Outer Space Treaty signed
by more than ninety countries, including the United States, and dangerously escalates the likelihood of a massive new arms race. The
treaty spells out that "The exploration and use of outer space . . . shall
be carried out for the benefit of and in the interests of all countries."
The treaty affirms that space should be used only "for peaceful
purposes."

In November 2000, 163 countries voted in favour of a United
Nations General Assembly resolution on the Prevention of an Arms
Race in outer space, reaffirming the Outer Space Treaty and its provi-
sion that space be reserved for peaceful purposes only. Only the U.S.,
Israel, and some small U.S.-dependent Pacific islands abstained. *Pax
Christi*, the Catholic journal, wrote:

> Canada has been highly active in seeking to strengthen the Outer
> Space Treaty. Their representative at the UN said "There is no

---

* *Socialist Standard.*

question that the technology can be developed to place weapons in outer space, but, if one state actively pursues the weaponization of space, we can be sure others will follow."

Late in 2002, the House of Commons Standing Committee on Foreign Affairs recommended that the Canadian government should continue to oppose the weaponization of outer space.[*]

Yet, today, the Martin government continues to pretend that the NMD has nothing to do with the weaponizing of space, and is intentionally misleading the public before it makes its announcement that it plans to jump on board the Bush and Rumsfeld fantasy. And, where in the past DFAIT has shown deep concern about the dangers of the NMD, today DFAIT is an enthusiastic cheerleader.

Now let's turn to the U.S. Air Force Space Command's "Strategic Master Plan." Ernie Regehr writes

> The document details how the U.S. Air Force Space Command is developing exotic new weapons, nuclear warheads, and spacecraft to allow the U.S. to hit any target on earth within seconds. It also unashamedly states that the U.S. will not allow any other power to get a foothold in space.
>
> The first page of the document clearly spells out America's agenda. General Lance W. Lord writes in his foreword: "As guardians of the High Frontier, Air Force Space Command has the vision and the people to ensure the United States achieves space superiority today and in the future."[†]
>
> The strategy "will enable us to transform space power to provide our nation with diverse options to globally apply force in,

---

[*] Report, House of Commons, December 12, 2002.

[†] General Lord is Commander, Air Force Space Command, Peterson Air Force Base, Colorado. He is responsible for the development, acquisition, and operation of the U.S. Air Force's space and missile systems, and he oversees a global network of launch facilities and the combat readiness of American intercontinental ballistic missiles.

from, and through space . . . to give the U.S. military the capability to deliver attacks from space instantaneously across the face of the earth."

Regehr continues:

A list of strategies and objectives detail the goals of Space Command in the coming years. These include . . . a nuclear arsenal in space.

According to the *San Francisco Chronicle*:

Look up at the sky. Imagine space-based weapons orbiting the globe, ready to zap or nuke any country declared an imminent threat to the United States.

No, this is not science fiction. It is Defense Secretary Donald Rumsfeld's vision of global domination. . . .

Rumsfeld's dream is dangerous . . . It threatens to reignite the arms race, this time in space. . . .

Look up at the heavens. Do we really want to leave future generations with a legacy of space-based warfare?*

So, are there even the slightest doubts about U.S. plans to weaponize space? Not a tiny shred of a doubt. Extensive official Washington documentation makes it clear that Americans are now working on space weapons inextricably linked to NMD plans. In Douglas Roche's words:

Entry into U.S. missile defence equals the end of Canadian policy opposing weapons in space. We will be sacrificing [our efforts to] build peace and security through the development of international law.

Paul Hellyer, in his last book, says it well:

---

* Ruth Rosen, November 13, 2003.

That Canada may become an accessory to such a monstrous scheme sends shivers of disgust up and down my spine.[*]

The Union of Concerned Scientists spells it out:

> The international community notably including Russia and China, Canada and the countries of the European Union, supports a ban on weapons in outer space.
>
> The Outer Space Treaty stipulates that "The exploration and use of outer space shall be guided by the principle of co-operation and mutual assistance . . ."

Anyone who might somehow still be skeptical about American plans for space will have any remaining doubts removed by going to the United States Space Command's "Vision for 2020,"[†] a sixteen-page document signed off by U.S. Air Force General Howell M. Ester, Lieutenant-General Edward G. Anderson, Major General David Vesely, and Rear Admiral K.A. Laughton.

> U.S. Space Command – dominating the space dimension of military operations . . . . Integrating Space Forces into warfighting capabilities across the full spectrum of conflict.
>
> The emerging synergy of space superiority will lead to Full Spectrum Dominance. Space power will be . . . decisive in war, and preeminent in any form of conflict. Increased weapons lethality will lead to new operational doctrine . . . space superiority is emerging as an essential element of battlefield success and future warfare. There will be a critical need to control the space medium to ensure U.S. dominance on future battlefields.
>
> Control of space is . . . an ability to deny others the use of space,

---

[*] *One Big Party*, Chimo Media, 2003.

[†] See Appendix Two for internet site.

the fourth medium of warfare. [Included will be] Robust negation systems and Space-based strike weapons.

Commenting on the American "Vision for 2020" document, Science for Peace says

The principle of using space-based weapons is clearly presented .... There is no ambiguity to "Space-based strike weapons" as part of the plan for the Global Engagement Capabilities. In the chapter on "Space Command" a graphical depiction of what control of space means is presented.

There can be no doubt that the U.S. plans to use space as another medium for warfare. In the plans that have been made public, the U.S. has clearly articulated its intention to place weapons systems in space.

Bear in mind that these plans are not secret, they are not vague. They are public, detailed, and specific. According to U.S. Air Force General (Ret.) Ronald Fogleman:

Space in and of itself is going to be very quickly recognized as the fourth dimension of warfare.

And, more recently, in a news report from Ottawa, February 7, 2004

The Pentagon will proceed with developing a space-based interceptor starting next year, a move that appears to undermine claims by Canadian officials that the proposed U.S. missile shield has nothing to do with putting weapons into orbit.

The U.S. plan to develop space weapons could prove to be a problem for Canada's participation. Prime Minister Paul Martin reiterated in the Commons on Thursday Canada opposes weapons in space and the country will not take part in the U.S. system if it involves such capabilities.

Meanwhile, Foreign Affairs Minister Bill Graham again said "This issue has nothing to do with going into space . . . The present plan has nothing to do with the weaponization of space."

David Pratt, who is supportive of Canada joining the American program, has said the possibility the system might lead to weapons in space is "so far off into the future that it's not a concern for us at this point."*

Right, way off in 2007 to 2010, as clearly indicated in the published U.S. timetable.

I have a question for you. Given the pious, reassuring statements we have had from Paul Martin, Bill Graham, John McCallum, and David Pratt, given the *overwhelming* evidence that the U.S. intends to aggressively weaponize space, are there again only three possible conclusions? My own conclusion is that either these men are incompetent, or they are very poorly informed, which I do not for a moment believe, or they have been deliberately misleading Canadians.

Seven years ago, in a 1997 speech, the American Assistant Secretary of the Air Force for Space, Keith Hall, made the U.S. position clear in a speech to the National Space Club. "With regard to space dominance, we have it, we like it, and we're going to keep it." According to *Pax Christi*,

> The NMD is not defensive; it is an integral part of the U.S. Space Command with its motto "To dominate and control the world from space." The Space Command's Long Range Plan states: "Achieving space superiority during conflicts will be critical to U.S. success on the battlefield." Space Command Commander in Chief Gen. Joseph Ashy said in 1996, "Some people won't want to hear this, but absolutely – we're going to fight in space. We will engage terrestrial targets – ships, airplanes, land targets – from space.†

---

* David Pugliese in the *Ottawa Citizen* and *Edmonton Journal*.

† October 2001.

Speaking to British parliamentarians soon after Donald Rumsfeld issued his space commission report before joining the Bush government, Karl Grossman of the Commission on Disarmament, Education, Conflict Resolution and Peace of the International Association of University Presidents and the United Nations, said

> The Bush administration would have the world believe this is about "missile defenses." This is untrue. A broad U.S. space military program is involved. Space is becoming the center of gravity for the Department of Defense. The plans are to "control space" and to "dominate space."*

Forgive me for repeating some of the words you've just read about the American plans to weaponize space, while adding a few new ones: "There can be no doubt," "clearly articulated," "no ambiguity," "control space," "dominate space," "space superiority," "apply force in, from, and through space," "the capacity to deliver attacks from space instantaneously," "a full spectrum of space dominance." Keep these words in mind the next time you hear Paul Martin, Bill Graham, or some other government official, speak on the subject.

Before we go on to the next chapter, here's former Liberal minister of defence, Art Eggleton, on the NMD plans:

> I do not see why anybody would be against having that kind of system. That kind of system is not star wars. It does not lead to an arms race. It does not lead us down the path of weaponizing of outer space.†

---

* Karl Grossman is the author of *The Wrong Stuff: The Space Program's Nuclear Threat to Our Planet* (Common Courage Press, 1997) and the video *Nukes in Space* (EnviroVideo). See www.envirovideo.com.

† House of Commons, May 3, 2001.

And, once more, Foreign Affairs Minister Bill Graham, who for many is quickly losing all remaining credibility:

> We owe it to ourselves to be accurate about what is at stake. . . . Sovereignty . . . is what this discussion is all about. . . . We will enhance the security of our people. . . . It is not about Star Wars. . . . There is no suggestion that this plan has anything to do with measures against Russia, or destined against Russia or China. . . . Weapons in space is not a policy of U.S. missile defence. . . . Let us not be hallucinating over star wars when it does not exist. . . . Weaponization of space is not something that Canada will be part of. . . . The U.S. program will not lead to an arms race. . . . This system is exclusively a defensive system and has no offensive capacity. How can that contribute to the arms race? . . . Non-proliferation, arms control, and disarmament remain pillars of our foreign policy. . . . The missile defence program we are discussing with the United States is not about star wars. It is consistent with our commitment to disarmament and the containment of weapons of mass destruction. . . . We are ensuring that we are not headed for the weaponization of space. . . . In every conceivable forum, Canada has said that we do not believe it is in the interests of the United States, or any country, to weaponize space, that this would be a disastrous mistake. I have said it. My predecessors have said it. We have said it at the United Nations. We have stated it 100 times.[*]

Now, back to David Pratt, speaking in the House of Commons the same day:

> We have gone to great lengths to encourage informed discussion on missile defence.
>
> As far as we know, there may and likely never will be any space-based weapons. We should not even be engaged in that sort of speculation . . . .

---

[*] House of Commons, February 17, 2004.

Some have said that the missile defence system will not work. This is certainly not our preliminary assessment . . . .

Some have said that the missile defence system would encourage other countries to build more and better missiles, thus sparking an international arms race. There has been absolutely no evidence of this to date. In fact, the evidence seems to discount this argument entirely.

All of this talk of star wars is not true. Canadians by now should know that it is not true.

Some have attempted to confuse Canadians by referring to missile defence as star wars. This is a false characterization and it only takes away from informed and honest debate.

The missile defence system . . . does not involve in any way weapons in space.

Canada continues to oppose the weaponization of space. We have made this very clear to the United States.

Well, it again truly boggles the mind. Judge for yourself.

The very same day that Graham and Pratt said these words in the House of Commons, the Washington-based *Air Force Print News*, under the headline "Space integrates air force to win wars," reported that

Integrating space into all operations – air, land and sea – is the future of Air Force Space Command, said Gen. Lance Lord during a symposium . . . .

"I want to talk about the integration of air and space, land and space, and sea and space. We see it coming together now in ways we never thought. . . ."

"Space is an indispensable partner in the American way of waging war."

One day later, on February 19, 2004, the Washington-based Center for Defence Information under the title "USAF Transformation Flight Plan highlights space weapons," said

For the first time in recent history, the U.S. Air Force has formally published a list of planned space weapons programs.

The plan, dated November 2003, but only recently posted on the Air Force Web site (www.af.mil) . . . makes it clear that space weapons are indeed envisioned as part of the future U.S. arsenal – and further that technologies to enable these weapons systems are now being researched and developed, including destructive kinetic energy missiles and laser space-strike weapons.

Deployment is planned beginning in 2010, and will include "Hypervelocity Rod Bundles which will provide the capacity to strike ground targets anywhere in the world from space."*

Of most concern . . . is the fact that the U.S. military is proceeding down a path toward space weaponization in what is essentially a public policy vacuum, with enormous strategic implications.

Leonard David, senior space writer for SPACE.com elaborates on this theme:

The U.S. Air Force has filed a futuristic flight plan, one that spells out the need for an armada of space weaponry and technology for the near-term and in years to come.

The use of space is highlighted throughout the [176-page] report, and includes discussions of space global laser engagement, anti-satellite missiles, weapons with the capability to strike ground targets anywhere in the world from space, rapid attack systems, a Space Operations Vehicle that can guide and dispense conventional weapons, sensors and other payloads worldwide from and through space within one hour of tasking.

---

* Elsewhere, the Center for Defense Information describes these "Rods from God" as bundles of tungsten rods fired from orbiting platforms, hurtling toward Earth at 3,700 metres per second, accurate within a range of eight metres and able to destroy even the most hardened targets. They could be launched at only a few minutes' notice, at any target on the planet.

The public document is described by the Air Force as "a road map for the future." The road map spells out the use of space to locate and track targets anywhere on earth.*

The following extracts from "Transformation Flight Plan," an official U.S. Air Force report, is quite clear about U.S. intentions. The full document is available from the Center for Defense Information Web site, www.cdi.org.

Overview of Capabilities

Taken together, space weapons provide a number of distinct advantages and disadvantages:

Advantages

Access and reach. Space weapons can attack targets that may be inaccessible to other weapons, could provide access to targets without concern for transit of denied airspace, and could provide global power projection to nations that possess them.

Rapid response. In contrast to weapons launched from ships or aircraft, which could take a few days to some weeks to reach a theater of operations far from the United States, space-based weapons could offer response times from several minutes to several hours. Only long-range ballistic missiles can achieve similar performances.

Distance. The great distance of space-based weapons from earth and from other objects in space have two key advantages. First, it makes space-based weapons less vulnerable to attack. Second, it would help distinguish them from terrestrial ballistic missiles carrying nuclear weapons.

Difficulty of defense. Space-based kinetic-energy weapons directed at surface targets are very difficult to defend against because of their very high velocity and very brief flight through the atmosphere. The difficulty is similar to that involved in defeating reentry vehicles from ICBMs but is complicated by the possibility of a much-shorter warning time.

---

* February 22, 2001.

According to the CDI, the Missile Defense Agency has requested funds "for improving the performance of all weapons by integrating space sensor platforms . . . using a space-based kinetic energy kill vehicle. Peter Teets, Air Force Undersecretary, says that among the five priorities that he has set for future space efforts are "warfighting" and "ensuring freedom of action in space.""*

CDI's vice-president Theresa Hitchens writes:

> The U.S. Air Force plans to turn space into the next battlefield, bristling with orbiting weapons designed to attack satellites, ballistic missiles and even targets on earth . . . a critical feature enabler of the pre-emptive strike strategy articulated by the White House.
>
> The Air Force Transformation Flight Plan details a stunning array of exotic weapons to be pursued over the next decade [including] "hypervelocity rod bundles (nicknamed Rods from God) designed to burst from space into the atmosphere at high speeds . . . weapons intended for offensive first-strike missions.†

In March 2004 the Center for Defense Information produced a long, detailed, and chilling document by Jeffrey Lewis, Executive Director of the Association of Professional Schools of International Affairs. The study, titled "What if Space Were Weaponized? Possible Consequences for Crisis Scenarios," shows how "the use of space weapons could lead to a rapid escalation of hostilities – possibly even to nuclear war." The document reminds readers that:

> Beijing and Moscow have pressed for negotiations in the Conference on Disarmament in Geneva on the issue of "preventing an arms race in outer space." The U.S. position has been that there is no space arms race currently underway and that negotiations are unnecessary.

---

* *Air Force Link*, Air Force Print News, March 26, 2004.

† *San Francisco Chronicle*, March 15, 2004.

Returning briefly to DFAIT (www.dfait-maeci.gc.ca) and to another of their absurd press releases, we learn that while "Russia initially voiced serious concerns over U.S. plans for BMD . . . Russia has been discussing BMD co-operation with the United States . . ."*

Theresa Hitchens of the CDI, writes

> Under the administration of President George W. Bush there has been increasing emphasis by U.S. government officials of the perceived need for the United States to prepare for eventual war in space. U.S. Space Command and Missile Defense Agency plans already envision the deployment of space-based weapons as integral parts of future U.S. arsenals.
>
> Even the U.S. Air Force's own space war games up to now have concluded that potential negative consequences from the use of space weapons – including the possibility of triggering a nuclear response from an enemy – cannot be dismissed.

The CDI document's Executive Summary makes two salient points:

> The Pentagon is moving forward with a number of research efforts to develop the capabilities to fight a war in, through, and from space, and yet there has been almost no public discussion of the costs vs. benefits of such a strategy.

And,

> In a world with space weapons, the United States may be better armed, but we may well be less secure.
>
> It is important to understand [that] . . . if the United States pursues these capabilities, other nations almost assuredly would too.

---

* January 15, 2004.

Contrast these words with DFAIT's constant refrain that in their attitude towards NMD:

> The Government is committed to ensuring and enhancing the security of Canada and Canadians.

Paul Hellyer puts it well:

> The notion that NMD will save Canadian lives is unquestionably the most far-fetched of all the arguments.[*]

On February 22, 2004, under the headline "Pentagon preps for war in space," the Center for Defense Information reported

> An Air Force report is giving what analysts call the most important detailed picture since the end of the Cold War of the Pentagon's efforts to turn outer space into a battlefield.
>
> For years, the American military has spoken in hints and whispers, if at all, about its plans to develop weapons in space. But the U.S. Air Force Transformation Flight Plan changes all that. Released in November, the report makes U.S. dominance of the heavens a top Pentagon priority in the new century. And it runs through dozens of research programs designed to ensure that America can never be challenged in orbit – from anti-satellite lasers to weapons that "would provide the capability to strike ground targets anywhere in the world from space."
>
> The Air Force report goes far beyond defensive capabilities, calling for weapons that can cripple other countries' orbiters.
>
> That prospect worries some analysts, who fear the U.S. may spark a worldwide arms race in orbit.

---

[*] Speech, May 15, 2002.

And, the following day the best journalist in Canada on the subject, David Pugliese of the *Ottawa Citizen*, under the headline "U.S. plan calls for launching weapons into space," told readers that

> The United States air force has unveiled a plan to put weapons into orbit and destroy other countries' satellites as part of a strategy that views outer space as dominated by America and its allies.
>
> The plan, which echoes former U.S. president Ronald Reagan's Star Wars scheme, proposes systems such as a space-based radio frequency weapons and anti-satellite missiles.
>
> Other weapons would involve putting mirrors into orbit so they can reflect laser beams against targets . . . and a system that would fire from space to hit targets on the ground.

Note that "airborne lasers" are being "developed for the Pentagon's missile defence shield." Pugliese's report on the Air Force Transformation Flight Plan continues:

> The ability to deny an adversary's access to space service is essential so that future adversaries will be unable to exploit space in the same way the United States and its allies can.
>
> Defense analyst Theresa Hitchens, vice-president of the Washington-based Center for Defense Information, says this system is significant in that it links the missile shield to missions involving the destruction of satellites owned by other nations.

Note *"it links the missile shield"* to weapons in space. A few days after this report was released, even more details emerged. In a seminar for senior U.S. air force leaders, the future use of space by the American military was addressed. General Lance W. Lord, said that they are "working hard on space control" to, if necessary, deny the use of space to others. Air Force Undersecretary Peter B. Teets, the Pentagon's executive agent for space, said the U.S. had to "maintain space dominance." General Lord

added that "Space superiority, along with air superiority, is our mandate."
According to *Air Force* magazine,[*] the Air Force is now "writing concepts of operations . . . about how to integrate manned and unmanned
platforms and space capabilities."

James W. Canan, writing in *Aerospace America Online*, leaves little
doubt:

> Among top-priority Air Force missions, controlling space is fast
> becoming as important as controlling the air.
>
> The nation has come to count on air superiority in war, and now
> must be able to count on space superiority as well, claim Air Force
> space officials. Many in the military space community believe that
> to achieve this, the U.S. will have no choice but to deploy weapons
> in space.[†]

Should any of this have come as any surprise to anyone? Hardly. U.S.
plans to weaponize space have been public knowledge for at least two
years, if not longer. Only Ottawa seems oblivious, or at least pretends
to be.

Terrence Edward Paupp, writing in Waging Peace.org sums it up
nicely:

> The technology for building a comprehensive national missile
> defense (NMD), in the true sense of the word "defense," is not avail-
> able. The technology for the deployment of NMD currently does not
> exist. Reoccurring test failures indicate that it is likely that the tech-
> nology will not exist in the future. Rather, the technology that does
> exist is for offensive purposes in outer space. What is currently
> available for deployment in outer space is a weapons technology
> capable of uniting the military, economic, and political compo-
> nents of a U.S. strategy for the hegemonic dominance of the globe.

---

[*] *Air Force* magazine, vol. 87, no. 2.

[†] *Aerospace American Online*, February 22, 2004.

The militarization of space, as proposed by the advocates of NMD, represents a radical departure from established international laws and customs, which historically have guided international relations on earth. The U.S. military-industrial complex and certain corporate and financial interests, which guide many aspects of U.S. government decision making, have decided that planning and preparation for aggressive war is going to be the most effective way to govern the planet. As expressed by U.S. Space Command's publication, "Vision for 2020," the goal of dominating the space dimension of military operations is "to protect U.S. interests and investment."

The goal of achieving the domination of the space dimension of military operations, with its central purpose of protecting U.S. interests and investments, is not a "defensive" position or purpose. Rather, the stated plan involves the militarization of space for aggressive purposes, aimed at rivals, anticipated revolts, and opposition to U.S. hegemony around the globe. As such, in violation of the 1945-Nuremberg Principles, the vision of U.S. Space Command, as well as its governmental and industrial supporters, constitutes "planning and preparation for war." In the language of the Nuremberg Principles, it constitutes "a crime against Peace."

More recently, from Philip Coyle, in a report by the *Toronto Star*'s Tim Harper from their Washington Bureau:

Coyle also said anyone who feels Canadian participation will lead to better protection for Canada misunderstands the system. "That's not in the cards . . ." But politicians in Canada who believe the system will be the first step towards weaponization of space are correct.[*]

And what about American plans for putting nuclear weapons in space? Loring Wirbel writes in his recent book *Star Wars: US Tools of Space*

---

[*] *Toronto Star*, March 17, 2004.

Supremacy,[*] that senior American officials have been talking about "space negation," i.e. denying others the use of orbital space, for years. As well, with the American Nuclear Posture Review of early 2002

> the Defense Department under Donald Rumsfeld has made clear that it wants to rely on nuclear weapons as another arrow in the quiver of space dominance.

Moreover,

> The U.S. will constantly insist on the right to military tools it will deny to all other nations worldwide.

The new U.S. goal will ultimately be "pre-emptive attack on other nations, and absolute dominance in orbital space." And now, note this:

> the entire purpose of multi-tiered missile defense is shifted to making pre-emptive space dominance more effective for the U.S. and those nations deemed its friends.

How can this have happened?

> The easy answer would point to the explicit empire-building favored by Rumsfeld and key Defense Department underlings like Richard Perle and Paul Wolfowitz.
> . . . the US Space Command had prepared the path for global domination with its "Vision for 2020" document in 1996 setting out the requirement that the U.S. control the planet by single-handedly controlling space.
> The right of pre-emptive planetary management is now virtually assumed by all Bush administration officials.

---

[*] *Star Wars*, Pluto Press, (www.plutobooks.com).

And, now this!

> Adding nuclear weapons to this volatile mix constituted the strate-
> gists' *coup de grâce*, and was easy to anticipate after the US Space
> Command and Strategic Command were merged in October 2002.
> All that was necessary was a strategic vision to unite the prospects
> for next-generation nuclear weapons, with the extant plans for
> conducting war in and from space.
>
> The ramifications of melding doctrines of pre-emptivity and
> space dominance are profound and multi-faceted. The unilateral-
> ists in the Bush administration have made clear their plans for con-
> ducting war around the globe using the medium of space.

On April 29, 2004, David Ruppe of Global Security Newswire in
Washington, D.C., reported that the U.S. Missile Defense Agency:

> is planning for an early 2006 test . . . that critics said would set an
> unwanted precedent for using space-based weapons.

According to Theresa Hitchens, "You will have just busted the taboo
against shooters in space."

Other American critics said that the planned test would clearly
establish a precedent for the weaponization of space with obvious capability for offensive antisatellite warfare. The Center for Defense
Information quotes a senior government official who says "We're cross-
ing the Rubicon into space weaponization."[*]

In view of all the abundant official evidence about U.S. plans, what
can one say about the *absurd* denials of Paul Martin, Bill Graham, and
David Pratt? What I say yet again is that there's *no* other conclusion to
make: all three have been misleading Canadians.

---

[*] NMD@cdi.org, May 11, 2004.

THE BUSBOY AT THE CONVEYOR BELT
INSIDE THE TENT

Clearly this is an escalation of the arms race. This is a lunacy program. It cannot be justified from a defence point of view, nor from an economic point of view.

> – Alex Shepherd, Liberal MP,
> House of Commons, February 17, 2004

If they weren't so dismaying, the following words from Paul Martin would seem perfect for a *Royal Canadian Air Farce* or *This Hour Has 22 Minutes* satire. In answer to a question during his first televised town hall meeting after becoming prime minister, Martin said

> I don't want to see a situation where American missiles are flying over Canadian airspace in order to attack some rogue missile coming in and we have nothing to say about it. I want to make darn sure that if that kind of activity is going to take place, first of all, that it doesn't take place over Canadian . . . in our air, over Canadian airspace.

Peter Mansbridge then asked:

Do you really think that we'd have a say if there was an incoming missile coming over our territory towards the United States, that they would wait to see whether or not we wanted them to knock it down?

Paul Martin replied:

Well, we would certainly have more of a say than if we weren't at the table at all.

In his CBC town hall forum, Martin repeated his mantra about having to be "at the table" three times.[*] We have to be "at the table to know what's going on so we can influence the final decisions." Or as other Liberals have put it, "We have to be inside the tent." But, is there really *anyone* who seriously believes that "being at the table" would in any way alter American plans, or make Canada safer?

Or, even if we were to actually join the American NMD plans, is there a single soul who believes that we would in any significant way have some influence over U.S. plans to weaponize space? Or their plans to develop a new generation of nuclear weapons? What about the argument that the Americans are going ahead with their program anyway, so we best be at the table in case we can influence things to our benefit?

Try this for size. In a statement last June, U.S. Air Force Secretary James Roche said that U.S. allies would have "no Pentagon veto power" over projects designed to achieve American military control of space. After all, Donald Rumsfeld's Pentagon is convinced that the struggle to control space will be the next stage of a coming global arms race.[†]

We keep hearing from Americans that we Canadians don't spend enough on the military. Every recent American ambassador to Canada

---

[*] February 6, 2004.

[†] A Pew Research Center poll asked, "To what extent do you think the United States takes into account the interests of other countries when making international policy decisions?" Seventy-three per cent of Canadians said, "Not much" or "Not at all." *New York Times*, June 27, 2004.

apparently assumes that Canada is essentially a colony, and proceeds to ignore diplomatic etiquette while publicly berating our country for not pouring billions of extra dollars into defence, and, of course, into the bank accounts of U.S. defence contractors such as Boeing, Northrop Grumman, Raytheon, and Lockheed Martin (all intricately involved with Bush's Star Wars plans).

Meanwhile, in poll after poll after poll, year after year, Canadians put increased defence spending far down the list of national priorities behind health, education, and more dollars to fight child poverty. They also say quite emphatically that they don't appreciate the likes of Ambassador Paul Cellucci telling us we have to increase our defence spending. (Most recently, as I write these words, in a speech to the Toronto Board of Trade, Cellucci once again criticized Canada for not spending enough on the military.)[*]

Today, the U.S., with 44 million men, women, and children who have no health care insurance, and another 48 million with hopelessly inadequate health insurance, and with one of the three-highest child poverty rates among the thirty OECD countries, spends more on their military than the next twenty-five countries put together.[†] Juxtapose this with the absurd suggestion that if Canada spends billions more on defence, we will somehow then be able to influence U.S. military, defence, and foreign policies in any meaningful way.

This year the U.S. will spend almost $450 billion on military activities or over $51 million an hour. Does anyone for a moment believe that if Canada increased our annual defence budget by 1 per cent of that

---

[*] In the 2003 Centre for Research and Information on Canada (CRIC) annual *Portraits of Canada* polls published in January 2004, 73 per cent of Canadians said increased health care spending should be a high priority, 67 per cent opted for more education and training spending, while only 30 per cent wanted Ottawa to spend more money on the military.

[†] Jim Stoffels points out that only 5 per cent of the U.S. military budget would lift every American child up out of poverty. Meanwhile, U.S. "defense" spending has increased by two-thirds between 2000 and 2004.

amount (an amount we clearly cannot afford) that this would give us an important say about U.S. policies?

As for the argument that being inside the tent would give us access to important new technology, Tariq Rauf, formerly of the Monterey Institute of Strategic Studies in Monterey, California, writes "To believe that the U.S. would share its latest high technologies in this field with allies is akin to believing in the tooth fairy!"

MP John Godfrey said it very well in the *Globe and Mail* last August after a big battle in the U.S. Senate:

> If the weaponization of space cannot be stopped on the floor of the U.S. Senate, why would we presume to believe that we can have a significant effect on NMD's direction? Canadian proponents of NMD often proclaim that we need to be at the table. But there is no table – only a conveyor belt passing us by.

Earlier, also in the *Globe and Mail*, Paul Hellyer wrote

> Only the most naïve of Canadians would suggest that being at the table . . . would give us one iota of influence. This is one of the most spurious of arguments.*

Perhaps *Toronto Star* columnist Tom Walkom's summary is the most succinct:

> There is little advantage being at the table when you're the busboy.

As for the argument that not signing on to the American Star Wars plans will result in the U.S. turning its back on Canada, or that they will punish us, Tariq Rauf, in a paper on "Canada's Perspectives on NMD," points out that Canada and the U.S. are currently "enmeshed in more

---

* *Globe and Mail*, May 15, 2003.

than 300 military agreements and treaties." It's interesting to keep this in mind when considering the vacuous threats that Canada would be "cut off" if we don't participate in the NMD plans.

Our current agreements with the U.S. are hardly one-way; the U.S. would never have signed them if they were. Among the arrangements already in place, as listed by Rauf who is now in Geneva at the IAEA, are joint planning and operations, combined exercises, defence production, logistics, communications, research and development, and intelligence sharing. "In addition, there exist approximately 145 bilateral forums involving regular consultations, discussions and meetings." As well, "over 20,000 visits are conducted annually to the U.S. by Canadian government and industry representatives related to defence activities."

Moreover, there are numerous long-established and valued boards and committees, some over sixty years old, such as the Canada–United States Permanent Joint Board on Defence which meets twice a year, the Canada–United States Military Cooperation Committee, the Canada–United States Regional Planning Group, etc., and the new Canada–U.S. Binational Planning Group. If anything, defence against terrorism post-9/11 makes this co-operation even more valuable to the U.S. than before. During the lifetime of most of these agreements there have been numerous important disagreements with the U.S. on foreign and defence policy, yet co-operation in most areas continued uninterrupted.

As for the oft-repeated contention by Liberal politicians in Ottawa that we have to be at the table to gather more information before we make a decision, a DFAIT news release on January 15, 2004, told us

In accordance with the 1994 Defence White Paper, Canada has held regular consultations on Ballistic Missile Defence (BMD) with the United States and other allies in recent years, both bilaterally and through the North Atlantic Treaty Organization (NATO). Canada and the United States established a BMD Bilateral Information Sharing Working group that has met twice a year since 2000. In addition, Canada placed a Canadian Forces Liaison Officer with the U.S. Missile Defense Agency in early 2001 for the purpose of supporting the ongoing consultation and information exchange process.

The Government entered into discussions with the United States on possible Canadian participation in BMD after years of consultations.

So, we've *already* been at the table with the Americans on the question of BMD for at least four years. Despite all their earnest protestations to the contrary, isn't it clear that the Liberals already know exactly what the U.S. is planning? And isn't it obvious that they made up their minds long ago that they wanted Canada to join the BMD scheme?

Are there many Liberal MPs who oppose the Prime Minister's plans to join the NMD program? Many Canadians were encouraged by the fact that thirty Liberal MPs supported the February Bloc Québécois motion calling on the government to end negotiations with the U.S. Altogether, seventy-one MPs supported the Bloc motion. Some of the Liberals made very valuable points. MP Alex Shepherd zeroed in on who is going to be in charge.

It is clear to me that this so-called partnership is really not a partnership at all. We talk about the ability of Canada to sit at the table. The American military attaché in the embassy came here one day and made it very clear that they were not going to run this through NATO or NORAD, that it would be run through the Northern Command. It will be entirely under U.S. command. We therefore do not really have a seat at the table at all. We will be told what to do.

This is not my idea of a partnership. This is the hypothesis of the argument that we have to be involved with them because it will give us a say. I do not think we have a say at all. What we will have to give up and what the cost will be to Canada will be our independent voice in international affairs, something that is respected around the world.

Shepherd was followed in the House of Commons by Charles Caccia

> Does Canada have an enemy to be concerned about and if so, who is
> the enemy? We know there are potential threats posed to the U.S.
> administration but certainly those threats are not posed to Canada.
> Therefore it would seem to be desirable that in this debate one should
> draw a line between the position of Canada and the position of the
> U.S. administration. These are two completely different situations.
>
> If Canada were to join a missile defence system, then the possi-
> bility would become very strong that Canada would attract this
> potential enemy to include our territory as a target. There is very
> little doubt that we would be seen as part, as other members have
> indicated, of a continental approach that would therefore make
> Canada part of an initiative that emanates from the U.S. adminis-
> tration. I see actually in Canada's interest an initiative that would
> decouple Canada from any defence system for North America for
> the very simple reason that Canada does not have any enemy to be
> worried about. Therefore Canada does not need to set up a system
> of defensive missiles that one day could become offensive.

Winnipeg Liberal MP John Harvard contributed this:

> I think what the Americans want from us more than anything is
> our stamp of approval. They want to say, "Hey, look at those good
> Canucks, those good, innocent, freedom-loving, peace-loving
> Canadians. If they can support missile defence, it cannot be all
> bad, can it?"*

Shepherd was more direct.

> Once again I would like to state my unequivocal opposition to
> Canada proceeding with a ballistic missile defence.

---

* Harvard was appointed Lieutenant-Governor of Manitoba in May 2004.

Where I come from, if the road sign says "weapons in space," we do not want to go down there because the likelihood is that when we get to the end of the road, that is where they will be.

Clearly this is an escalation of the arms race. This is a lunacy program. It cannot be justified from a defence point of view, nor from an economic point of view.

Charles Caccia summed it up nicely:

Canada's interests are best served by being at the disarmament rather than the armament table.[*]

---

[*] *Hansard*, February 17, 2004.

Rushing into a Gigantic Boondoggle, and the *Real* Threat

This extraordinary emphasis on missile defense represents mis-placed priorities. The top priority should instead be combating the threat of nuclear terrorism . . .

— Union of Concerned Scientists

Now let's turn to the question of whether there really is an ICBM missile threat. Richard Gwyn wrote in the *Toronto Star*:

It's impossible to imagine any circumstances in which some sui-cidal dictator would heave a nuclear missile at the U.S. – a feat that's exceptionally difficult to do in itself – while knowing that minutes later he himself would be vaporized in a mushroom-shaped cloud.

Terrorists are quite another matter. If and when they ever acquire weapons of mass destruction, they'll try to slip them in by ship or by truck. Against such a threat, the U.S.'s anti-missile program is irrelevant, which is to say it's a gigantic boondoggle.[*]

---

[*] *Toronto Star*, September 22, 2002.

Let's again suppose for a moment, ridiculous as it may be, that down the road, say twenty years from now, after many hundreds of billions and probably much more have been spent on a so-called missile shield, that the shield is at least moderately effective, a *huge* leap of faith in itself. The *Los Angeles Times* says "If you want to bring a nuclear weapon into the United States, just hide it in some shipment of illegal drugs."

The Union of Concerned Scientists says "nuclear weapons detonated in a U.S. port while still in a shipping container in a cargo ship" is another of the "delivery options . . . that would be less expensive." And in relation to 9/11 and the destruction of the World Trade Center, in an incredibly scary suggestion,

> Had these attackers chosen to fly commercial aircraft into the nuclear power plants less than 10 miles upwind of New York City, it might have made the entire region an unlivable nuclear wasteland for generations.

As several writers have pointed out, since tons of cocaine are smuggled into the U.S. every year, what's to prevent a warhead or two, or more, being transported across the border? American military and Republican NMD advocates don't like to talk about this.

Paul Krugman has few doubts and agrees with a report published by the American Army War College that says that the war in Iraq has been a "detour" that has undermined the fight against terror. Both David Kay, the former UN weapons inspector and CIA adviser, and Richard Clarke, the long-time White House terrorism adviser, embarrassed and angered the Bush administration by publicly coming to the same conclusion.

There are those who say that September 11 makes the NMD program a necessity. I would think that it proves exactly the opposite. *The Economist* explains:

> The threat comes from terrorists; there are much cheaper, handier and less incriminating ways for weapons of mass destruction to be

dispatched by al-Qaeda, or a rogue despot, than by a ballistic missile – such as a suitcase. The billions being handed to the Missile Defense Agency could be better spent on humbler things such as port security . . .*

The Union of Concerned Scientists puts it this way:

This extraordinary emphasis on missile defense represents misplaced priorities. The administration's top priority should instead be combating the threat of nuclear terrorism by increasing its programs to keep nuclear warheads and materials out of the hands of terrorists. The Bush administration, however, is giving this problem a fraction of the attention and funding being given to missile defense. The missile defense system being rushed into deployment is not relevant to the war on terrorism.

A new nuclear risk has emerged. Thousands of so-called tactical nuclear weapons, some of which are small enough to be transported by a person, are stored in poorly secured locations in Russia. Nuclear materials that can be used to make nuclear weapons are even more poorly secured throughout the world. For example, scientific research reactors in dozens of countries are fueled with weapons-usable uranium.

Despite the end of the Cold War more than a decade ago, U.S. nuclear weapons policy remains mired in Cold War thinking.†

---

* December 6, 2003. In March 2004, it was reported that al-Qaeda are believed to have fifteen freighters under their control, ships that could be outfitted with chemical or nuclear bombs and sailed into a harbour and blown up. The *New York Times* reports (June 27, 2004) that "some 20,000 shipping containers a day arrive at United States ports, with perhaps 1 per cent inspected . . . . The Central Intelligence Agency is believed to have concluded that a crude atomic bomb or other terror weapon is far more likely to arrive in the United States via shipping container than on a missile from a rogue state."

† www.ucsusa.org/global_security

On February 4, Reuters quoted a Cairo report that al-Qaeda purchased as many as 100 "portable suitcase-sized bombs" from the Ukraine when Ukrainian scientists visited Kandahar in 1998.

Former Russia national security advisor Alexander Lebed said that as many as 100 portable bombs went unaccounted for when the Soviet Union dissolved. Mr. Lebed said each one was equivalent to 1,000 tonnes of TNT and could kill as many as 100,000 people.[*]

Kurt Gottfried is an emeritus professor of physics at Cornell University and a co-founder of the Union of Concerned Scientists. In a May 2003 article titled "A Ticking Nuclear Time Bomb," Gottfried addressed the question of terrorist access to nuclear materials, in particular highly enriched uranium (HEU) and plutonium.

The Russian stockpile holds about 1,000 tons of HEU. By contrast, less than 100 pounds of such uranium is needed to make a crude bomb of the type that destroyed Hiroshima, the design of which was so simple that it was not even tested by the United States before being used in 1945. It would only be prudent to assume that a capable terrorist group like al-Qaeda could build a weapon of this type if it could get enough HEU.

Perhaps worse, only a handful of plutonium is needed to make a weapon of the type that destroyed Nagasaki. The Russian stockpile has enough plutonium for thousands of such bombs. States that seek nuclear weapons for military use, especially as warheads for missiles, are therefore very eager to acquire plutonium.

Russia's nuclear weapons are better secured than its fissile materials and, on the whole, weapons are much harder to steal and transport. Still, the Russian stockpile does contain thousands of portable tactical nuclear weapons that are relatively "small" in size.

---

[*] *Globe and Mail*, February 9, 2004.

Knowledgeable sources indicate that many of the older models still in the stockpile are not equipped with locks that require a code or key to prevent unintentional use. Clearly, terrorists would have special interest in getting such a ready-to-use device.*

We also now know that Pakistani scientist Abdul Qadeer Khan has sold nuclear technology, including secret blueprints, centrifuges, and components for over a decade to such places as Malaysia, Sri Lanka, Turkey, Morocco, North Korea, Iran, and Libya. Is there much doubt that Osama bin Laden or his successors, not to mention other terrorists, will have had access to this information? In April 2004, his second-in-command, Ayman al-Zawahiri, boasted that al-Qaeda now possessed radioactive material combined with conventional explosives in the form of suitcase bombs, and that "anything is available for thirty million dollars on the black market in central Asia."†

Not only would defensive security measures concentrating on potential terrorist attacks be *far* more effective than the Bush/Rumsfeld NMD plans, they would not generate the escalating response from Russia and China and other nations now so badly frightened by America's space war plans.

I doubt that the public fully understands the hair-raising ramifications of Abdul Qadeer Khan's shocking activities. Even Mohamed ElBaradei was completely taken aback by how much equipment and how many detailed plans were spread so widely around the world, in what he called "a veritable Wal-Mart of black market proliferation" in Europe, the Middle East, Asia, and South Africa. Without question, the future now looks much more threatening.

What takes the breath away is the sheer scale, and the apparent ease with which it was done. Weapons blueprints (so Libya has

---

* www.ucsusa.org

† Carnegie Non-Proliferation Project, npp@celp.org, April 15, 2004.

admitted; the others aren't saying), materials and parts for thousands of centrifuges to enrich uranium from which bombs can be made, as well as for related nuclear processes, were bought, in effect by mail order, like so many assemble-it-yourself bookshelves or kitchen cabinets. Thoughtfully, there was after-sales service instructions: technical questions could be relayed back to the scientists at source, presumably in Pakistan where the whole illicit business originated. Middlemen operating from Europe, the Middle East, Africa and Asia were on hand to speed delivery and process payment.

If individuals, with or without an official nod, can organize the supplying, what is to stop other individuals doing the buying? And if money was the Pakistani scientists' main motive, Osama bin Laden has plenty of that.[*]

Dr. Abdul Qadeer Khan, the father of Pakistan's nuclear bomb, a much admired and revered man in his country, with the certain, though hotly denied participation of the Pakistani military and intelligence service, has set into place a situation where countries such as Iran and North Korea could (if they have not already) transfer the technology obtained from Pakistan to terrorist groups who would build nuclear weapons. Seymour M. Hersh, writing in *The New Yorker*, says that IAEA inspectors in Libya found precise blueprints for the design and construction of a half-ton nuclear weapon that will fit into a family car. "It's a terrorist's dream." Hersh goes on to tell of his conversation with Mohamed ElBaradei who said

I have a nightmare that the spread of enriched uranium and nuclear material could result in the operation of a small enrichment facility in a place like northern Afghanistan.[†]

---

[*] *The Economist*, February 7, 2004.

[†] March 8, 2004.

What about the wildly exaggerated idea emanating recently from a U.S. Library of Congress report that the threat of terrorism could come from Canada, because we are "hospitable to organized crime and terrorism"? Of course, as in all other Western nations, there are those in Canada with terrorist connections. And of course Canadians must be vigilant. But, University of Toronto security and intelligence expert Wesley Wark responds that the U.S. report seems to have been written by a person who

> didn't have a very good grasp of the realities of security policy in Canada. I found it a very unimpressive and very inexpert (and) a very crude look at the Canadian situation. I thought it was a dreadful piece of work ... very unbalanced.*

But, perhaps it is on a par with the splendid research the CIA, the FBI, and the U.S. National Security Agency managed in relation to the bountiful weapons of mass destruction that would surely be found in Iraq, and on a par with the hopeless work of the CIA and FBI prior to September 11.

In March, in a widely reported story from the right-wing Nixon Center think tank in Washington, the Canadian border was called "a preferred *jihad* access route to America." Europe and Canada were both harshly criticized for "indulgent" immigration and refugee policies. The report notes that "nearly all terrorists in the West have been immigrants." Of interest is the report's conclusion that of 212 terrorists examined, by far the largest number were in the U.S. and had not originated in Canada. (Among Nixon Center board members are such objective "notables" as Henry Kissinger and Conrad Black.)

No doubt Canadians have to remind Americans, yet again, that there were more than six million illegal aliens in the U.S. at the time of 9/11, and that thirteen of the nineteen hijackers entered the U.S. legally on student, tourist, or business visas.

---

* *Toronto Star*, February 17, 2004.

Oh, and by the way, no Canadian flight training school was dumb enough to agree to train applicant pilots who had no interest in learning how to takeoff or land a plane.

We now know that George W. Bush ignored intelligence information and explicit warnings from Bill Clinton before 9/11, and that, according to Richard Clarke who served three U.S. presidents as the White House counterterrorism expert,

> By invading Iraq, the President of the United States has greatly undermined the war on terrorism.*

David Rennie of the *Daily Telegraph*, writing from Washington, says

> Clarke described an administration in which a small circle of hawks fed Bush only what they wanted him to hear. Bush "ignored it; he ignored terrorism for months."†

Instead Bush, Rumsfeld, Condoleezza Rice and Deputy Secretary of Defense Paul Wolfowitz (described as an "Iraq Hawk") were obsessed by Iraq, while Clarke and others said the focus should be prompt action against al-Qaeda. After 9/11 Bush demanded that officials "go back over everything" to "see if Saddam did this . . . if he's linked in any way . . . I want to know any shred." We also now know that after 9/11 a bipartisan delegation urged Bush to spend about $10 billion on important security priorities such as at U.S. ports and nuclear sites, but the president rejected their pleas.

More recently, two American defence and security analysts wrote:

---

* Testimony to Congress, March 24, 2004. Perhaps Clarke's most ominous speculation is the possibility of a "Taliban-like" government in Pakistan as a result of the U.S. invasion of Iraq.

† *Daily Telegraph*, March 22, 2004.

... if defeating terrorism remains the top U.S. security goal, why is the Bush administration spending billions on major weapons systems more appropriate to the Cold War? Why maintain 12 aircraft-carrier battle groups and fund new nuclear-powered attack submarines and three fighter-plane programs?[*]

In November of 2001, in a letter addressed to the U.S. Senate Majority and Minority Leaders, the Speaker of the House of Representatives, and the House Minority Leader, the Federation of American Scientists, including fifty Nobel Prize winners in chemistry medicine, physics, and economics, wrote

In the interest of national security we urge you to deny funding for any program, project, or activity that is inconsistent with the Anti-Ballistic Missile (ABM) Treaty. The tragic events of September 11 eliminated any doubt that America faces security needs far more substantial than a technically improbable defense against a strategically improbable Third World ballistic missile attack.

Regarding the probable threat, the September 11 attacks have dramatized what has been obvious for years: A primitive ICBM, with its dubious accuracy and reliability and bearing a clear return address, is unattractive to a terrorist and a most improbable delivery system for a terrorist weapon. Devoting massive effort and expense to countering the least probable and least effective threat would be unwise.

In May 2003, Professor Richard Schneider, President of the Canadian Council of Churches, wrote to prime minister Chrétien and members of the Chrétien cabinet expressing concern about the government's intention to become involved in the U.S. BMD system. The letter urged the government to

---

[*] Sanford Gottlieb and Christopher Hellman, *USA Today*, March 22, 2004.

seek an unqualified commitment from the U.S. that ballistic missile defences will not involve basing or testing any weapons in space

and to request that

the United States government agree to talks in Geneva at the Conference on Disarmament leading to a space weapons ban, before proceeding further with BMD deployment.

Both requests were essentially ignored. Then, on March 15, 2004, the Canadian Council of Churches, including the Anglican Primate, the Canadian Conference of Catholic Bishops, the Moderator of the United Church, Baptists, Methodists, Quakers, Lutherans, Mennonites, Presbyterians, and many others, wrote to Prime Minister Martin urging

An intensified commitment to nuclear disarmament and binding controls over ballistic missiles as the most effective and practical means of working for the safety and protection of Canadians.

Proposed security solutions like ballistic missile defence fail to counter the nuclear threat and precipitate further insecurities.

We urge your government to unequivocally reject the expensive futility of ballistic missile defence. We call on you to focus on the more realistic pursuit of diplomacy and verification technology to mitigate the missile threat, and further, to encourage the United States to do the same.

Three days later Bryan Adams, Pierre Berton, Michael Ondaatje, David Suzuki, Susan Aglukark, Sacha Trudeau, Sarah McLachlan, Bruce Cockburn, Fred Penner, George Bowering, Flora MacDonald, Naomi Klein, Robert Bateman, and many other well-known Canadians sent an open letter to the Prime Minister urging him not to allow Canada to become involved in the U.S. administration's missile defence system, which will have long-term negative consequences for global security, and for Canadian sovereignty.

Eleven days later forty-nine U.S. Generals and Admirals, including three former Joint Chiefs of Staff, wrote to George W. Bush that

> U.S. technology already deployed, can pinpoint the source of a ballistic missile launch. It is, therefore, highly unlikely that any state would dare to attack the U.S. or allow a terrorist to do so from its territory with a missile armed with a weapon of mass destruction, thereby risking annihilation from a devastating U.S. retaliatory strike.

The letter ended this way:

> As you have said, Mr. President, our highest priority is to prevent terrorists from acquiring and employing weapons of mass destruction. We agree. We therefore recommend, as the militarily responsible course of action, that you postpone operational deployment of the expensive and untested NMD system and transfer the associated funding to accelerated programs to secure the multitude of facilities containing nuclear weapons and materials and to protect our ports and borders against terrorists who may attempt to smuggle weapons of mass destruction into the United States.

Yet Washington is plunging ahead, wasting tens of billions of dollars, while the real threat looms ominously. And our own Canadian military-industrial establishment is enthusiastically proclaiming "us too please!" Jeffrey Simpson writes

> Scared? You should be. A crazy, uncertain, dangerous world lurks out there. Pakistan's nuclear chief sells secrets to North Korea, Iran and Libya, only to receive a pardon from Pakistan's dictator-cum-

president, thereby furthering Pakistan's reputation as the world's most dangerous country.*

The Carnegie Endowment for International Peace says

In case after case, U.S. intelligence has uncovered proliferation, but other priorities took precedence. The clearest case was in the 1980s, when the United States ignored Pakistan's acquisition of nuclear capabilities because it needed Islamabad's help to fight the Soviets in Afghanistan. History is repeating itself, now that Pakistan is America's "ally" in the war on terror.†

Note that Pakistan now has between thirty and fifty nuclear weapons, then read Jeffrey Simpson above once more.

Meanwhile, in Washington, D.C., on March 30, Richard Clarke said that since 1999, both the Canadian Security and Intelligence Service and the RCMP have been "bending over backwards to be helpful to the U.S."** But he also indicated that the U.S. invasion of Iraq has radicalized Muslim youth "into heightened hatred of America," and given al-Qaeda an unprecedented recruitment opportunity. And of course this was before the photographs and details of the horrendous American treatment of prisoners in Iraq were revealed.

---

* *Globe and Mail*, February 7, 2004.

† *Key Proliferation Questions*, vol. 7, no. 6, March 24, 2004.

** *Globe and Mail*, March 31, 2004.

THE ROGUE NATION:
"NO LONGER TRUSTED . . . IT SHOULD BE FEARED."

For globalization to work, America cannot be afraid to act like the almighty superpower it is . . . The hidden hand of the market will never work without the hidden fist . . . And the hidden fist that keeps the world safe for Silicon Valley's technologies is called the U.S. Army, Navy, Air Force and Marine corps.
– Thomas Friedman, *New York Times Magazine*, March 1999

In my book *The Vanishing Country*, I referred to the United States as "a rogue nation." Although the book was very well received and went on to become a bestseller across the country, one reviewer chastised me for calling the U.S. a rogue country and said no one else was using such words. Since then several books and numerous articles about the U.S. have been titled *Rogue Nation* (Clyde Prestowitz) or *Rogue State* (William Blum), etc., most of them written by Americans.

A dominant theme in John le Carré's latest novel *Absolute Friends* is that current U.S. behaviour is a threat to world peace as great as the terrorism it is fighting. Le Carré refers to the Bush government as a "neo conservative junta," calls the war on Iraq "illegitimate . . . a criminal and moral conspiracy . . . no provocation . . . no links with al-Qaeda,[*] no weapons of Armageddon . . . It was an old colonial war dressed up as a crusade for Western life and liberty."

Linda McQuaig writes:

> Washington prefers to characterize its [missile] plans as defensive, just as it characterized its war against Iraq as defensive . . . In that sense its plans to rule the world with military might are also "defensive."[†]
>
> If only countries would stop resisting U.S. rule, there'd be no need to bomb them into submission.

An editorial in the *Toronto Star* on New Year's Day put it well:

> For the first time in almost 60 years, a major country has mounted a deliberate challenge to the authority of the United Nations and the international rule of law.

The American rule will be

> Washington will decide alone. American behaviour will destroy the international system of multilateral co-operation that has been the goal of statesmen since the founding of the United Nations.

Terrence Edward Paupp writes for the Nuclear Age Peace Foundation:

---

[*] How well-informed are Americans about foreign policy issues? Iraq is a very good example. In a national public opinion poll in the summer of 2003, just under 70 per cent of Americans said that they believed that Saddam Hussein was directly involved in the 9/11 destruction of the twin towers in New York. Needless to say, the U.S. administration did nothing to try to convince the public otherwise.

[†] In the 1969 Reith Lectures, former prime minister Lester B. Pearson said "The distinction between offensive and defensive arms is a very simple one. If you were in front of them, they were offensive; if you were behind them, they were defensive."

In retrospect, the crusade by the advocates of NMD signals a back-to-the-future scenario, repeating the same depleted arguments of the Reagan administration. Prospectively, the crusade by the advocates of NMD constitutes a vision of a United States that is disconnected from the rest of the world. In the words of William D. Hartung, the President's Fellow at the World Policy Institute at New School University, "the unifying vision behind the Bush doctrine is nuclear unilateralism, the notion that the United States can and will make its own decisions about the size, composition and employment of its nuclear arsenal without reference to arms control agreements or the opinions of other nations."*

George A. Lopez, Chairman of the *Bulletin of the Atomic Scientists*, says

Despite a campaign promise to re-think nuclear policy, the Bush administration has taken no significant steps to alter nuclear targeting policies or reduce the alert status of U.S. nuclear forces. Meanwhile, domestic weapons laboratories continue working to refine existing warheads and design new weapons . . .

The Bulletin also cited the continuing U.S. preference for unilateral rather than co-operative action, and U.S. efforts to impede international agreements designed to limit the proliferation of nuclear, biological and chemical weapons.†

In the February 17, 2004 debate in the Commons, former NDP leader Alexa McDonough reviewed some history.

In December 2003 the U.S. cast the only dissenting vote on the UN resolution for a comprehensive [nuclear] test banning treaty. In December 2003 it voted against the total elimination of nuclear

---

* www.wagingpeace.org

† www.thebulletin.org. The *Bulletin* was founded by several World War II–era Manhattan Project scientists and has warned about nuclear peril since 1945.

weapons. It voted against the obligation for nuclear disarmament again in December 2003, and abstained on a vote at the UN to prevent the weaponization of space. In fact, when the UN general assembly voted on a resolution, specifically the prevention of an arms race in outer space, on which well over 160 countries voted in favour, the U.S. opted to abstain.

This from *The Economist* in November 2003:

> The anxiety in both Europe and Asia is whether America is becoming so different from everywhere else that it is becoming a problem for the world, not a solution. It is not just a reckless Bush administration . . . the United States is now inherently assertive and unilateralist and can no longer be trusted to lead the world. [For many, instead] it should be feared.

Richard Gwyn writes in the *Toronto Star*:

> What is new is the readiness in Washington to act like Rome, unapologetically, unilaterally, ruthlessly.[*]

According to John R. MacArthur, publisher of *Harper's Magazine*:

> This administration is more narrow-minded, more ideologically driven, more hostile to international co-operation than any since Ronald Reagan's first term, back when the Cold War still raged.[†]

Zbigniew Brzezinski was U.S. President Jimmy Carter's national security adviser. In his new book *The Choice: Global Domination or Global Leadership*, he writes:

---

[*] *Toronto Star*, September 22, 2002.

[†] *Globe and Mail*, July 19, 2003.

U.S. credibility worldwide has been badly hurt by the WMD affair ...
[this is] indisputable. Numerous public opinion polls demonstrate
there has been a worldwide drop in support for U.S. foreign policy.
There is manifest resentment of recent American conduct and a
pervasive distrust of America's leaders.*

On March 5, 2004, the Associated Press reported on the results of a
survey:

A majority of people living in the two countries bordering the
United States and in five major European countries say they think
the war in Iraq increased the threat of terrorism in the world ...

The polls found that people living in all the countries except the
United States have an unfavorable view of the role that President
Bush plays in world affairs. Only in the United States did a majority, 57 per cent, have a positive view of the role played by the U.S.
president.†

Just over half in Mexico and Italy had a negative view of Bush's
role. In Britain, the closest U.S. ally in the war in Iraq, and in
Canada, two-thirds have a negative view.

Sam McGuire, director of opinion research at Ipsos UK, said
Bush's low ratings in Britain are notable, given that country's close
alliance with the United States. Britain traditionally has been seen as
the United States' "staunchest European ally on world affairs," he said,
and long has been a buffer between the United States and Europe.

Three-fourths of those in Spain and more than four in five in
France and Germany had a negative view of Bush's role in world
affairs.

---

* *Edmonton Journal*, February 9, 2004.

† By the summer of 2004, a CBS poll showed that only 41 per cent of Americans
approved of the job Bush was doing as president, 61 per cent disapproved of the way he
was handling Iraq, and 65 per cent said that their country "is on the wrong track."

In the poll, strong majorities believed that both the U.S. and Britain lied about Iraq, and said that they have lost confidence in Washington's trustworthiness. Former U.S. secretary of state Madeleine Albright said "The credibility of the United States is sinking and the numbers who believe that Bush and Blair lied to them is incredibly serious." For Paul Krugman in the *New York Times*:

> I think we're dealing with the most closed, imperialistic, nastiest administration in living memory. They even put Richard Nixon to shame.*

That's quite something to say, given that in the past the U.S. has propped up terrible, ruthless dictatorships in Chile, Greece, in Iran and in other countries. It has directly intervened and mounted covert operations in Guatemala, the Dominican Republic, Panama, Haiti, Somalia, Nicaragua, El Salvador, Ecuador, Colombia, Cuba, and elsewhere. It armed Saddam Hussein and trained the Taliban at a CIA camp in Virginia. It is by far the largest weapons exporter in the world, and has by far the largest stockpile of weapons of mass destruction, nuclear, chemical, and biological, and the most advanced, sophisticated means of delivering them.†

Which country is now committed to spending billions of dollars to develop a new generation of nuclear weapons? Which country has by far the largest stockpiles of ICBMs? Which country is now in the process of reassessing its use of nuclear weapons with a view to employing them as an alternative to conventional bombs? In which country is there increasing speculation about the efficacy of nuclear warfare and nuclear attack options complementing other military operations? Which country has increased spending on nuclear weapons in 2004 by more than 50 per cent? And which country has a plethora of senior military

---

* January 16, 2004.

† *The Vanishing Country*, McClelland & Stewart Ltd., 2002, pages 240-241.

strategists that regard missile defense as part of "a splendid first-strike capability"?* California Senator Dianne Feinstein says "The Bush administration is moving towards a military posture in which nuclear weapons are considered like other weapons."

As for the so-called bunker busters that the Pentagon is now planning to develop, the Union of Concerned Scientists has this to say:

> Even a small, low-yield earth-penetrating nuclear weapon will create enormous fallout. The radioactive debris thrown into the air can drift for miles on the wind. The use of these weapons would lead to severe collateral damage . . . and enormous amounts of fallout from dirt and debris carried into the air which will then fall back to the ground. Even a one-kiloton nuclear warhead that explodes 20 feet underground would eject about one million cubic feet of radioactive debris from a crater the size of ground zero at the World Trade Center.

In plans made public in 2002, the Bush administration spelled out its National Strategy to Combat Weapons of Mass Destruction, a document that says that the U.S. has the right to use nuclear weapons preemptively, even against a country that doesn't have them. For the Union of Concerned Scientists:

> Ironically, this policy conveys a clear message to present and future adversaries of the United States: Spare no effort to acquire nuclear weapons, since this is the only way weaker states can deter U.S. intervention.

So, the U.S. goes to war in Iraq, ostensibly because of the threat of weapons of mass destruction, while at the same time it is developing a whole new arsenal of weapons of mass destruction. In May 2003, the U.S. Senate voted to repeal their 1993 legislation that banned research

---

* Ritt Goldstein, www.atimes.com, May 5, 2004.

and development of low-yield nuclear weapons and also approved research into new high-yield nuclear weapons many times more powerful than the bombs that decimated Hiroshima and Nagasaki.

It's clear today that Bush and Rumsfeld want to begin nuclear testing again. One hundred and seventy nations have ratified the Comprehensive Test Ban Treaty (CTBT), but the U.S. administration has let it sit unpassed in the Senate, which means the treaty cannot enter into force since the U.S. is a requisite state. It's also clear that the U.S. has no intention of complying with its commitments under the Non-Proliferation Treaty, with the certain result that other countries will escalate efforts to acquire nuclear weapons.[*]

As for the American abandonment of the ABM Treaty, the former head of the Russian National Security Council told an international conference that this action "will result in the annihilation of the whole structure of strategic stability," while Russian Defence Minister Igor Sergeyev said it "will trigger a new spiral in the arms race and ruin the existing system of arms control."

What colossal American hypocrisy! Keep all of this in mind the next time you hear George W. Bush, Colin Powell, Donald Rumsfeld, Dick Cheney, or any other American official use the words "weapons of mass destruction." Or the next time you hear Paul Martin, Bill Graham, or Stephen Harper tell you there's no need to be concerned about a new arms race. Ernie Regehr quotes Mohamed ElBaradei:

> The U.S. government insists that other countries do not possess nuclear weapons. On the other hand, they are perfecting their own arsenal. I do not think that corresponds with the treaty [the Nuclear Non-Proliferation Treaty] they signed.[†]

---

[*] The 1968 Treaty on the Non-Proliferation of Nuclear Weapons said "Each of the Parties of the Treaty undertakes to pursue negotiations in good faith on effective measures relating to cessation of the nuclear arms race at an early date . . ."

[†] Regehr quotes Brazil's President Luis Inácio Lula da Silva: "Why is it that someone asks me to put down my weapons and only keep a slingshot while he keeps a cannon pointed at me?"

Not only does U.S. policy include the concept of pre-emptive strikes, which has become a foreign policy doctrine, but this dangerous, destabilizing new policy now forms the basis of current Pentagon policy and is, to a large degree, what the National Missile "Defense" scheme is all about. According to Harvard strategic specialist Thomas Schelling, the U.S. has moved from a policy of deterrence to a doctrine of compulsion.

In October 2003, Noam Chomsky, in an article called "Dominance and its Dilemmas," wrote

> The imperial grand strategy is based on the assumption that the U.S. can gain "full spectrum dominance" by military programs that dwarf those of any potential coalition, and have useful side effects. . . .
>
> As the grand strategy was announced on September 17, the administration "abandoned an international effort to strengthen the Biological Weapons Convention against germ warfare," advising allies that further discussions would have to be delayed for four years. A month later, the UN Committee on Disarmament adopted a resolution that called for stronger measures to prevent militarization of space, recognizing this to be "a grave danger for international peace and security," and another that reaffirmed "the 1925 Geneva Protocol prohibiting the use of poisonous gases and bacteriological methods of warfare." Both passed unanimously, with two abstentions, the U.S. and Israel. U.S. abstention amounts to a veto: typically a double veto, banning the events from reporting and history.
>
> A few weeks later, the Space Command released plans to go beyond U.S. "control" of space for military purposes to "ownership," which is to be permanent, in accord with the Security Strategy. Ownership of space is "key to our nation's military effectiveness," permitting "instant engagement anywhere in the world. . . . A viable prompt global strike capability, whether nuclear or non-nuclear, will allow the United States to rapidly strike high-payoff, difficult-to-defeat targets from stand-off ranges and produce the desired effect . . . [and] to provide warfighting commanders the ability to

rapidly deny, delay, deceive, disrupt, destroy, exploit and neutralize targets in hours/minutes rather than weeks/days even when U.S. and allied forces have a limited forward presence," thus reducing the need for overseas bases that regularly arouse local antagonism.

Similar plans had been outlined in a May 2002 Pentagon planning document, partially leaked, which called for a strategy of "forward deterrence" in which missiles launched from space platforms would be able to carry out almost instant "unwarned attacks." Military analyst William Arkin comments that "no target on the planet or in space would be immune to American attack." . . . The world is to be left at mercy of U.S. attack at will, without warning or credible pretext. The plans have no remote historical parallel. Even more fanciful ones are under development. . . .

The new grand strategy authorizes Washington to carry out "preventive war." [Preventive, not pre-emptive.] Whatever the justifications for pre-emptive war may sometimes be, they do not hold for preventive war, particularly as that concept is interpreted by its current enthusiasts: the use of military force to eliminate an invented or imagined threat, so that even the term "preventive" is too charitable. *Preventive* war is, very simply, the "supreme crime" condemned at Nuremberg.

That is widely understood. As the United States invaded Iraq, Arthur Schlesinger wrote that Bush's grand strategy is "alarmingly similar to the policy that imperial Japan employed at Pearl Harbor, on a date which, as an earlier American president said it would, lives in infamy." FDR was right, he added, "but today it is we Americans who live in infamy."*

So what if the United Nations Charter forbids pre-emptive strikes? (Article 51 forbids the use of military force except for self-defence in response to armed attacks or if the Security Council authorizes military action.)

---

* www.zmag.org

In *The Vanishing Country*, I listed the many multilateral treaties and agreements that Canadians support, and in some cases helped initiate, but that the U.S. rejects.* I also quote the editor of *Foreign Policy* magazine, Moises Naim, who says

> no country is doing more to undermine the multilateral approach to issues of global concern than the United States.

And, as far as Canadian-American relations are concerned, columnist and author Lawrence Martin says

> Few American governments have been so inimical to Canadian interests as the government of George W. Bush.

Summing up, it's difficult not to be very angry about George W. Bush. He supports a policy of pre-emptive or preventative war. He has cancelled the vitally important ABM Treaty. He has moved towards replacing a non-nuclear-weapons policy with a new policy where nuclear weapons would be considered no different than conventional weapons. He has shunned multilateral arms control agreements and international law. A February 2004 editorial in the Fort Wayne *Journal Gazette* put it this way:

> The speech Bush delivered Wednesday at Washington's National Defense University was years late. The threat of nuclear proliferation has grown more dire since he took office and the problem can be traced to the leader of the world's premier nuclear power.
>
> The president conveniently refused to address complaints about the indifference, bordering sometimes on contempt, that the United States has shown for diplomatic attempts to stop nuclear proliferation.

---

* *The Vanishing Country*, McClelland & Stewart Ltd., 2002, page 233.

In an article called "Rogue State? Which State?" the writer asks the following questions:

(1) Which state is the world's leading producer and marketer of weapons of mass destruction, but is prepared to go to war against any state that possesses or is thought to possess some (provided it has only limited capacity to hit back)?

(2) Which state has exported half of all weaponry exports in recent years?

(3) Which state has single-handedly brought negotiations on the Biological Weapons Convention to a halt and walked away from the Convention on the Prohibition of Landmines; and undermined the UN conference on small arms?

(4) Which state has fatally undermined the Strategic Arms Reduction Treaty (START II) by leaving the 1972 ABM Treaty?

(5) Which country refused to join the International Criminal Court because of My Lai, the use of cluster bombs, the use of depleted uranium and a long list of other "illegal and immoral acts"?

(6) Which is the only country to have used nuclear weapons?

(7) Which country is years in arrears on its payments to the United Nations?

(8) Which country is the world's leading producer of greenhouse gases and consumer of oil, but refuses to sign the Kyoto protocol?

(9) Which country? The world's only true rogue state, the mighty U.S. of A.[*]

The *Atlantic* magazine[†] advises its readers that among all the world's developed countries the U.S. is in the bottom three with the worst records in poverty, economic inequality, infant mortality, homicide, health care coverage, and a host of other social indicators. The United

---

[*] Insane Planet, "Rogue State, Which State?"

[†] January–February 2003.

Nations says that in their list of twenty-four "high human development countries," the U.S. has the highest level of abject poverty. Let's consider all of this in the context of the words of former U.S. president Dwight D. Eisenhower:

> Every gun that is made, every warship launched, every rocket fired signifies, in the final sense, a theft from those who hunger and are not fed, those who are cold and are not clothed. This world in arms is not spending money alone. It is spending the sweat of its laborers, the genius of its scientists, the hopes of its children. This is not a way of life at all in any true sense.*

Dr. James L. Hecht makes this point:

> Perhaps most important we can improve the image of the United States by directing some of the money spent on unneeded weapons at increased foreign aid. The United States spends less on foreign assistance as a percentage of gross national product than any other industrial nation – less than one-third that of Germany, one-fifth that of France and one-ninth that of Denmark.†

For world-famous psychiatrist and author Dr. Robert Jay Lifton, one of the founding members of the Nobel Peace Prize-winning International Physicians for the Prevention of Nuclear War, the Bush administration "is special in its radical approach to the world . . . a dimension that is exaggerated and very extreme," countering terrorism with "poor responses that would paradoxically make the world more unsafe and the danger of terrorism even greater."**

So, which do you think would be the most effective means of decreasing the threat of future terrorist attacks, the National Missile

---

* 1953 speech to the American Society of Newspaper Editors.

† Philadelphia Newspapers Inc., September 9, 2000.

** Christopher Dreher, *Globe and Mail*, February 21, 2004.

Defense scheme, or following Hecht's suggestion? And who wants to bet that George W. Bush and Donald Rumsfeld would ever make such a dramatic, sensible change in direction? Mel Goodman, writing in *Foreign Policy in Focus*,* says

> The fall of the Soviet Union handed the U.S. a unique opportunity as the surviving superpower, to lead the world toward a period of greater co-operation and conflict resolution through the use of diplomacy, global organization, and international law. This great opportunity is being squandered, as the world becomes a more dangerous place. Military force is now looming larger than ever as the main instrument and organizing principle of U.S. foreign policy. In our new national security doctrine, in the shape of our federal budget, and in the missions of the agencies the budget funds, our government is being reshaped to weaken controls on its use of force and further incline our country toward war.
>
> Since the 2000 election . . . diplomacy has been shamefully abused. Led by Defense Secretary Donald Rumsfeld, the Department of Defense has moved aggressively to eclipse the State Department as the major focus of U.S. foreign policy, abandoning bipartisan policies of arms control and disarmament crafted over the past four decades.
>
> As a result the long-term security interests of the U.S. have been imperiled, weakening the international coalition against terrorism and compromising the pursuit of arms control and counterproliferation.
>
> Despite marked decline in the strategic threat to the U.S. since the collapse of the Berlin Wall in 1989, the Warsaw Pact in 1990, and the Soviet Union itself in 1991, military influence over national security policy has grown substantially, and congressional support for the Pentagon has never been greater. The influence of the military has led to the Senate's defeat of the Comprehensive Test Ban

---

* *Foreign Policy in Focus*, vol. 9, no. 1, February 2004.

Treaty; the abrogation of the Anti-Ballistic Missile Treaty (ABM), the cornerstone of deterrence for 30 years; U.S. rejection of the International Criminal Court and the ban of the use of land mines.

The doctrinal policies of the Bush administration have helped to make the international arena a more dangerous place. In his commencement address at West Point in June 2002, President Bush endorsed pre-emptive attacks, and several months later, the White House issued its National Security Strategy, which discarded the policy of détente and containment and endorsed pre-emptive or preventive military actions against states with which the U.S. is at peace.

Is the U.S. military and industrial complex firmly in control in Washington? Could there be any more blatant and appalling evidence of this than the announcement by Colin Powell that the United States "will give Pakistan easier access to military weapons . . . which would allow it to buy controversial depleted uranium ammunition and receive U.S. government financing to obtain weapons."* What a horrible combination: a terribly unstable country that already has nuclear weapons and missiles, plus sheer American lunacy and unmitigated greed.

Let's turn again to the words of Ambassador Westdal:

> The U.S. alone deploys some 12,000 weapons with an average yield of 20 Hiroshima-sized bombs. That amounts to some 240,000 Hiroshimas. At any given moment, there are some 7000-7500 operational warheads, some 2,300 of which are on alert, with power plenty enough to blow all of us and much else to kingdom come.†

---

* *Los Angeles Times*, March 18, 2004.

† March 2000. In June 2004, the Arms Control Association, aca@armscontrol.org, estimated that the current U.S. nuclear force amounts to approximately 10,000 warheads and that Russia now deploys "roughly 5,000 strategic nuclear warheads out of an estimated arsenal of some 20,000 total nuclear warheads."

For financier and philanthropist George Soros:

> The reckless pursuit of American supremacy has put us and the rest of the world in grave danger.*

Roger Morris worked in senior positions on the staff of the U.S. National Security Council under presidents Johnson and Nixon. He is an award-winning investigative journalist and historian. On May 25, 2004, *Common Dreams* reported Morris's comments about George W. Bush and his administration. He said the U.S. now has "the worst foreign policy regime by far in the history of the republic . . . a government that has flouted treaties and alliances, alienated friends, multiplied enemies, lost respect and credibility on every continent."

Remember, this is the government that both Paul Martin and Stephen Harper want to cozy up to. How is all of this directly connected to the American BMD and Star Wars plans? *Common Ground* staff has put it together well:

> Nearly 25 years ago U.S. Air Force Lt.-Col. Robert Bowman said that a ballistic missile defence (BMD) was "the missing link to a first strike." Bowman directed the search for such a system during the Jimmy Carter presidency, when he described the U.S. government's original motivation for developing the BMD.
>
> So why is the U.S. interested in attaining a first strike capacity without retaliation? First strike involves mounting a surprise attack using nuclear weapons, aimed at defeating an enemy by knocking out its weapons before they can be fired. Under U.S. presidents Nixon, Carter and Reagan, nuclear war strategies were developed aimed at achieving the capacity to mount an unanswerable first strike against the Soviet Union.†

---

* *The Bubble of American Supremacy*, Public Affairs, 2004.

† www.stopwar.ca

So, there you have it, the real truth without the misleading spin. It's *not* National Missile Defense. It's *not* Ballistic Missile Defense either. Its real name should reflect its real purpose, Global Missile Offense, or, if you prefer, Star Wars.

THE FOOLISH AND ARROGANT BUSH DOCTRINE

"Either you're with us or you're against us . . . Over time it's going to be important for nations to know they will be held accountable for inactivity."
— George W. Bush, Washington, D.C., November 6, 2001

How should Canada respond to George W. Bush's foolish statement that "either you're with us or you're against us"? Does that mean that we Canadians have to go along with all U.S. defence, military, and foreign policy strategies, proposals, and policies? If it does, then obviously we have to tell Americans that we can't possibly accept such a doctrine, that the entire basis for the Bush declaration is inherently flawed, poorly thought out, and quite unacceptable.

Ambassador Cellucci keeps threatening Canada about the serious repercussions if we don't go along with U.S. policy. The Americans might have to "tighten the border." As I wrote in *The Vanishing Country*:

> Oh dear! With a tightened border, how would we ever be able to ship Americans all that oil, natural gas, and electricity they are so desperately dependent on us for? And what about the fact that for

decades Canada has been the number-one destination, ahead of all other countries, for U.S. exports? Is Mr. Cellucci suggesting that a tightened border would work only one way?

More recently, the ambassador suggested that if Canada decriminalizes marijuana, the U.S. will have to take protective action at the border, and the consequences would be severe.

Well, Canadians have always believed in reciprocity. Why don't we respond to Mr. Cellucci by our taking action at the border in relation to the insanely gun-ridden and violent American society? After all, many thousands of handguns and other dangerous weapons are smuggled into Canada from the U.S. every year. Maybe we'll just have to photograph and fingerprint all Americans entering Canada, and carefully search their luggage. Surely Americans won't mind a few more lineups. After all, Mr. Cellucci, which is more dangerous, a few joints or some deadly handguns? And, by the way, haven't twelve American states already taken steps to decriminalize the possession of marijuana?

If we Canadians make the terrible mistake of joining the American NMD program, won't that have a profound effect on our sovereignty, on our ability to ever again have independent foreign and defence policies? What will happen to our long-standing efforts to promote disarmament? What will happen to our role in strengthening agreements opposing the weaponizing of space? What will happen to our role as strong supporters of peace and international law, and what will happen to the world's perception of Canada as an independent, peace-loving country? And, what will happen to our claims that

> Canada respects and fulfills its international non-proliferation obligations, and will continue to do so. The Nuclear Non-Proliferation Treaty forms the foundation of Canada's nuclear disarmament and non-proliferation policy. Canada continues to play an active role in strengthening this cornerstone of strategic stability.*

---

* See the DFAIT Web site: www.dfait-maeci.qc.ca

Some would argue that our joining the NMD program would be a simple extension of our NORAD agreement. But, former foreign affairs minister Lloyd Axworthy says that the end result would be a substantial erosion of Canadian sovereignty.

That's what always happens. The reality of any joint operational command is that the Americans always run the show.

The Liberal government will try to sell Canadians on the idea that NORAD involvement in the BMD plans will give Canada an important say in American military policy. This is pure nonsense. In reality, it will be the U.S. Strategic Command in Omaha, the U.S. Northern Command, the U.S. Joint Chiefs of Staff, the American Missile Defense Agency, and the Pentagon in 100 per cent control. Some Canadians from the continentalist right say that if we Canadians don't join Washington's Star Wars plans, we'll be isolated. But recent Pew Global Attitude polls show that it is the United States that is increasingly isolated. Foreign approval of America has plummeted dramatically since the election of George W. Bush. A February 5, 2004 *New York Times* report says

> Margaret D. Tutwiler, in her first public appearance as the State Department official in charge of public diplomacy, acknowledged Wednesday that America's standing abroad has deteriorated to such an extent that "it will take us many years of hard, focused work" to restore it.
>
> Edward P. Djereijian, a former ambassador to Israel and Syria, said that "The bottom has indeed fallen out of support for the United States." Even in countries that have friendly government relations with Washington, the image of America has fallen and "American prestige has dwindled."

Rather than leaving us isolated, Canadian rejection of the BMD will leave us much more respected in the world community of nations. Late in 2003, Lloyd Axworthy wrote:

There's good reason to think that support for BMD would curtail Canada's foreign-policy options. In fact, it would entail an abrupt change in our policy on the non-proliferation of missiles and weapons of mass destruction, moving from a model of multilateral regulation and co-operation to a confrontational approach based on the threat of force. This in turn would change the way Canadian foreign policy is regarded in other countries. We'd risk losing our still-considerable reputation as an independent supporter of multilateral institutions and the international rule of law – with potentially serious consequences for our global security and economic interests.

Do we have security obligations as North Americans? Of course we do. Ernie Regehr puts it in the right perspective:

> Canada's security obligations to the United States are serious, and throughout the Cold War Canada met its strategic security obligations. . . .
>   Even without missile defence co-operation, air defence co-operation and naval co-operation would continue.[*]

But nuclear buildups and the weaponizing of space are an entirely different matter. Policies which escalate tension in the world, and sharply diminish security and lead to the proliferation of weapons of mass destruction are an entirely different matter. Aggressive militarization and the abandonment of international arms control agreements are an entirely different matter.

George W. Bush's "with us or against us" doctrine is foolish in the extreme and the Canadian government should make this clear to the White House, the State Department, and the Pentagon.

At the end of every year, *Maclean's* magazine publishes the details of

---

[*] On April 15, 2004, contrary to the distortions emanating from Ottawa, Major General Raymond Rees, Chief of Staff for the U.S. Northern Command and NORAD, said that it would not mean the end of NORAD if Canada didn't join the U.S. NMD plans. NORAD would still have "a significant role to play."

an Allan Gregg public opinion poll. In the year-end 2003 edition, most of the poll was inexplicably missing. Here are some of the poll results that didn't appear in the magazine.

Asked "How would you describe our relations with the United States? Are we like family to each other, the best of friends, friends, but not especially close, cordial but distant with each other, or openly hostile and unfriendly?"

4% said Like family to each other.
10% said The best of friends.
45% said Friends, but not especially close.
32% said Cordial but distant.
5% said Openly hostile and unfriendly.

Compared to the 2001 and 2002 polls, far fewer Canadians answered "Like family" (10 per cent in 2001) or "Best friends" (23 per cent in 2001). In 2003, almost twice as many Canadians answered "Cordial but distant" compared with 2001.

When asked if their perception of the United States had become more positive or more negative, only 12 per cent said more positive, while 49 per cent said more negative. Two out of three who felt more negative towards the U.S. blamed "actions and policies undertaken by the Bush administration."

Asked about the war in Iraq, 75 per cent said we were right to stay out of the war, "even if it has annoyed our closest trade partners," while only 21 per cent said that we should have joined the U.S. in the war. In late April 2004, eight out of ten Canadians said that they did not think George W. Bush was necessarily a friend of Canada or knows anything about Canadian issues.[*] Then, in their May 3, 2004 issue, *Maclean's* magazine reported an exclusive Pollara poll which showed that America's global reputation has worsened during the past decade; fewer than one in ten respondents thought that it had improved. Forty-nine

---

[*] Ipsos-Reid poll, *Globe and Mail*, April 30, 2004.

per cent of Canadians said that the U.S. is a bullying or dangerous country, and the most frequent word used to define the U.S. was "arrogant." According to Pollara chairman Michael Marzolini, "we've never seen results this negative."

Here are five other very interesting polls, the third a disgusting example of appalling journalism.

First, in 1998, an Angus Reid poll found that 92 per cent of Canadians wanted the federal government to play a leading role in banning nuclear weapons. Perhaps you might want to ask our Liberal and Conservative leaders and MPs how we could ever do that if we join the American Star Wars plans.

And in the second poll (which should be of particular interest to the likes of Ambassador Cellucci), Ekos showed in December 2002, that 65 per cent of Canadians said that the "U.S. has no business telling Canadians to increase defence spending."

And now, from the *National Post*, an astonishing display of irresponsible journalism. On February 11, the *National Post* headlined a story by their Ottawa Bureau Chief Robert Fife, "Canadians want missile defence: poll." Immediately below the headline was a subhead that read "7 out of 10 in favour." Later in the story we read that "64% of Canadians favour missile defence."

The survey was by Pollara Inc., chaired by long-time Liberal pollster Michael Marzolini. Anyone reading this story will have no doubt that a strong majority of Canadians believe that we should fully participate in the American program. For example, according to an article by Dalhousie political scientist Frank P. Harvey in the *Globe and Mail* on February 25, 2004

> A recent Pollara poll showed that seven out of ten Canadians support missile defence. Critics of the program who obviously had hoped for greater public opposition, must be worried.
>
> Critics of BMD have lost the debate . . .

One small problem. No such question was asked in the survey, and no such answers were given! The words "National Missile Defence" appeared nowhere in the questions asked. Nor was there any other reference of any kind to missile defence. Yet the headline on the story was "Canadians want missile defence: poll." The supposed "fact" that 70 per cent of Canadians support the NMD plans has been repeated frequently in the House of Commons by both Liberal and Conservative MPs, and has been often cited in newspaper articles, columns, and editorials.

But, what can you expect from the *National Post*, the paper that wanted Canada to go to war in Iraq and today (May 1, 2004) still hopes Canada will send troops to Iraq to "send a message of friendship to the United States."

For the extreme, radical right-wing, and continentalist *Post*, there's no holding back. "Go ahead: Weaponize space" was the title of the lead editorial, February 26, 2004. Canada should stop dithering and overcome its "strange phobia of all weapons extraterrestrial." As well, it's "good news" that American missiles will likely be placed on Canadian soil since "the shield will protect our cities from attack no less than America's." As for the dangers of an arms race, Beijing and Moscow are not concerned.

According to Bill Graham, speaking about NMD plans in the House of Commons on April 27, 2004: "Our concern is what Canadians want." Excellent! One month earlier an Ipsos-Reid poll showed that 69 per cent of Canadians disagreed with the statement that "Canada should actively support the Bush administration's missile defence system even if it may require dedicating military spending to the program or allowing U.S. missile launchers in Canada." So, instead of a mythological 70 per cent of Canadians favouring the U.S. missile defence plans, just under 70 per cent are opposed. Quite a difference! Try as I might, I have been unable to find any mention of the Ipsos poll in the *National Post*.

Lastly, a U.S. poll, also released in March, said that only one in five Americans were in favour of proceeding with a missile defence system now, while 65 per cent were in favour of a new treaty banning all weapons in space, twice as many as those opposed to such a treaty.[*]

---

[*] The Program on International Policy Attitudes, March 16–22, 2004.

NATIONAL MYTHOLOGICAL DEFENCE: PROFITS AND GREED LINING THE POCKETS OF DEFENCE CONTRACTORS

The largest corporate welfare scheme in the history of the world.
— Seattle Weekly, 2000

. . . the history of the program is fraught with failure, fraud and coverup . . . it is difficult to credit the true believers with protecting anything more than the profits of the weapons industry.
— Jim Stoffels, 2003

Some Canadians believe that if the Democrats were to defeat President Bush in the November 2004 presidential election, our worries about U.S. NMD plans would be over. Perhaps, but it's wise to remember that in the 2000 presidential election, both Bush and Democratic nominee Al Gore backed the Pentagon's NMD plans, and in 1999 John Kerry voted in the U.S. Senate for missile defence deployment.

Two years later, speaking on the floor of the U.S. Senate on May 2, 2001, Kerry talked about Saddam Hussein's weapons of mass destruction and the need for the U.S. to develop a boost-phase anti-ballistic missile system, with a commitment by the Bush government to invest "the considerable resources to make these systems capable of reaching the speeds required to intercept an ICBM." Of course, that would mean amendments to the ABM Treaty, while understanding the inevitable Russian concerns, since "a fearful, insecure Russia is a dangerous Russia." But in the end, there can be no doubt that the U.S. "can continue [its] leadership by exploiting our technological strength to find a defense against ballistic missiles."

On the surface, it seems hard to understand. Why, in the face of all the abundant damning evidence, might an elected Democrat support such ill-conceived, illogical, and dangerous plans? James L. Hecht, formerly of the Center for Public Policy and Contemporary Issues at the University of Denver, explains:

> But if NMD is not needed, why does it have the support it does in Washington? The answer: skillful lobbying for unneeded weapons by military contractors who contribute large sums to political campaigns – the same reason that the United States is building a fleet of new attack submarines, at a cost of $3 billion each, to counter a next generation of Soviet submarines which will never exist.*

And should the Democrats be successful in the November 2004 presidential election? Dr. James Lindsay, Senior Fellow Foreign Policy Studies at the Brookings Institution in Washington, has no reservations:

> Despite their misgivings, the Democrats will not oppose NMD because to speak against "defending America" would be committing electoral suicide.†

Or, as David Nyhan says:

> No one gets elected to the House or Senate by telling voters, hey sorry, but there's no way to really protect your condo from nuclear attack.**

---

* Philadelphia Newspapers Inc., September 9, 2000.

† Halifax foreign policy round table, June 15, 2001.

** Nyhan is a columnist for the *Boston Globe*.

In 1998, the Nuclear Age Peace Foundation made it clear who stands to benefit:

> Ballistic missile defenses as envisaged by the U.S. are unilateralism in its most egregious form.
>
> Those who stand to gain the most from deployment are U.S. defense contractors, such as Lockheed Martin, Boeing, Raytheon and TRW. These corporations will reap tremendous profits. Ballistic missile defenses have so little potential value for security that one might conclude that profit and greed are the primary motivating factors in promoting them.*

According to Jim Stoffels,

> The NMD testing program has been structured to eliminate independent oversight and give unprecedented authority to companies like Boeing, Lockheed Martin, Raytheon, Orbital Sciences Corporation, and Northrop Grumman Corporation, which stand to make billions of dollars on the decision to deploy a system that does not exist and cannot work.†
>
> National missile defense in the United States is not a technology, it has been observed, but a theology. Given that the history of the program is fraught with failure, fraud and coverup, it is difficult to credit the true believers with protecting anything more than the profits of the weapons industry.**

In the summer of 2000, U.S. religious leaders including Baptists, Jews, Episcopalians, Mennonites, Methodists, Catholics, and others, wrote to President Bill Clinton:

---

* Nuclear Files.org

† In 2003, the top three U.S. defence contractors received over $50 billion in contracts, with Lockheed Martin heading the list at just under $22 billion.

** *Tri-City Herald*, January 24, 2003.

We write to inform you that we have come to believe that deployment of a national missile defense system would be a grave error. Instead of defending our nation against intercontinental missiles, at best a deployment decision will squander billions of public funds ... and, at worst, deployment may put the American people and the rest of the world in jeopardy of a new and more chaotic nuclear arms race.

Having carefully studied proposals for a NMD, the expert information and analyses persuade us that neither the security of our nation state nor the welfare of our people will be served. We will say what elected officials dare not say: only those who have contracts to build the NMD will benefit.

Our first line of defense is to reduce the nuclear threat and to build common security among nations, best achieved through arms control and multilateral diplomacy.

In short, the National Missile Defense is indeed a National "Mythological" Defense because it protects us against a bogeyman threat, could not accomplish what it promises to do, dismisses human need in favor of the profits of the few, puts in jeopardy treaties that protect us all, and will almost certainly provoke other nations who will be threatened by it.

The *Harvard Political Review*, under the title "The Star Wars Lobby: A Decade in the Making," goes right to the point:

Few realize that the recent debate over National Missile Defense (NMD) represents the culmination of a sophisticated lobbying effort dating back to the 1980s. After the Reagan administration failed to implement its Star Wars plan, staunch believers and desperate defense contractors turned their energies toward the immediate creation of an NMD lobby that has since served to shape the tone of the debate. By the time the issue gained major national attention this past summer, the debate had already shifted so much to the pro-NMD right that opposing it seemed to be opposing the very safety of America.

Immediately after the Reagan years, several members of the President's former staff began to build a network of support for NMD. For years defense contractors were able to quietly donate money. $200,000 donations to leading political figures were not infrequent.

Rep. Dennis J. Kucinich reacted with exasperation. "This isn't going to defend anything except the interest of some defense contractors and the lining of their pockets."[*]

For Web writer Donavan Hall:

In the absence of any clear opposition to National Missile Defense stateside, the Republicans will probably get their way and get rich doing it. I guarantee you that as billions of dollars are poured down the toilet of Star Wars, health care, welfare and other social services will be scaled back.

Arthur Terry, in the *International Herald Tribune* wrote

Republicans should appreciate business enough to believe in cost-effectiveness. Thus, applied to missile defense: 1) It costs enough to otherwise save untold lives through education and health; 2) like a Maginot Line, it is ridiculously easy to get around with a ship in a U.S. port, or a container smuggled in; 3) it is sure to start an arms race costing billions; 4) the "defense" does not even work. Conclusion: Cost high, effectiveness zero.

And, in the same paper, Joseph Fitchett advised:

Prominent physicists who know much about the mechanics of motion are quick to point out that building a functional NMD is physically impossible for a number of very fundamental reasons.

---

[*] *Harvard Political Review*, June 1, 2001.

This fact doesn't bother the Republicans who are only interested in securing the contracts for their corporate sponsors. As long as the military industrial complex can line its coffers with taxpayer gold, the Republicans will have succeeded in their "moral" mission.[*]

In 2000, Geov Parrish wrote in the *Seattle Weekly*

The National Missile Defense – the newest name for Star Wars – is now 17 years old. The idea of using missile-based systems to defend the U.S. against incoming missiles is over 40 years old, with an estimated price tag of over $125 billion in those years. After the latest test failure, national defense has exactly zero to actually show for that $125 billion.

Think about that for a moment. Think of the staggering amount of technological change that swept the world in the last 17 years. When Reagan took office, microwave ovens were just coming into common household use. More people still listened to AM than FM radio stations. Not only was there no known treatment for AIDS but the term "AIDS" did not yet exist for the dimly known "gay cancer." At the launch of "Star Wars," personal computers hardly existed – let alone laptops, let alone e-mail, let alone chat rooms, let alone the World Wide Web or the Internet or anything dot-com.

A lot has changed in 20 years. But we are no closer now than we were then to the impossible dream that is Star Wars. And the sum of money that has been shoveled out to military contractors – the true purpose of Star Wars – is a scandal so large that it may well represent the largest corporate welfare scheme in the history of the world.

The *Christian Science Monitor* is equally perceptive in a column by David R. Francis entitled "Hidden defense costs add up to double trouble."

---

[*] *Spinocracy*, vol. 1.7, February 19, 2001.

To measure actual spending by the United States on defense, take the federal budget number for the Pentagon and double it.

That's the "rule of thumb" advocated by economic historian Robert Higgs. . . .

[Doubling the requested $401.7 billion President Bush requested for the Department of Defense would make a total of some] $800 billion out of a total federal budget of $2.4 trillion.

With many numbers still unavailable, Higgs hasn't finished his calculations for fiscal 2004. But doubling the budget request won't overstate the truth by much, he says.[*]

The power of U.S. defence contractors in the American political systems has been demonstrated and recited in detail almost every year, and most certainly during election years. Unquestionably, this is one of the two most important reasons that the U.S. continues to pour so many badly needed billions into such an unpromising venture. (The General Accounting Office report released in early May 2004 pointed out two missile defence programs with a cost overrun of $400 million in 2003, another that was $1 billion over budget in a single year, and another that was more than a year behind schedule and between a half a billion dollars and a billion dollars over budget.)

According to Terrence Edward Paupp

The U.S. Space command and the Bush administration have continued to work in collusion with the civilian and military sectors dedicated to achieving the goal of "global engagement" that "combines global surveillance with the potential for a space-based global precision strike capability."

Meanwhile, Canadian defence industry officials met with representatives of the Pentagon in Ottawa in March "to see what opportunities" there might be for Canadian companies. Also present were the giant U.S.

---

[*] www.csmonitor.com, February 23, 2004.

defence contractors with subsidiaries in Canada. Anyone familiar with the high-powered lobbying skills of the Canadian Defence Industries Association and the Aerospace Industries Association of Canada, and of course the CCCE, will not be surprised by how often the phrase "potential industrial benefits" comes up and is stressed in testimony before the Commons and Senate Defence Committees. Ron Kane of the Aerospace Association notes how "very successful," his group has been "in the past supporting U.S. military programs," and Norbert Cyr of the Defence Industries group says "Obviously, if Canada were to become involved . . . I think that would create a more favourful climate."*

(It may come as a surprise to many Canadians that Canada has a multi-billion dollar international arms export industry substantially supported by our government in Ottawa. This said, U.S. arms exports between 1998 and 2002 were 41 per cent of total exports, compared to 0.8 per cent for Canada. U.S. arms exports were almost equal to those of Russia, France, the U.K., and Germany combined.)†

But, to focus solely on the funding of politicians by the defence contractors, and vice versa, as the prime reason for NMD fiscal, security, defence, and foreign policy folly is a mistake. Bush and Rumsfeld are not engaged in creating a "shield" to defend North America. What they are planning is an offensive first-strike, pre-emptive space weapons colossus intended to dominate the world for as far as we can imagine into the future.

As I am writing these words, Canada is in a well-justified uproar across the country over the disgusting $100 million Liberal sponsorship scandal. Yet I can't help thinking that in the United States well over $100 *billion* has been "poured down the toilet of Star Wars" with virtually not a peep out of the mainstream U.S. media, and with no discernable impact on public opinion or voting patterns.

In the House of Commons, David Pratt said allegations that the NMD system could cost as much as a trillion dollars were bad distortions

---

* CBC News, March 14, 2004.

† Pages 304 and 305, 2003 United Nations *Human Development Report*.

and Jack Layton and the NDP "owe the people of Canada the truth without trying to embellish this."* Responding to an NDP ad in the *Globe and Mail* that cited a possible trillion dollar cost, Pratt said "There is absolutely no basis in fact for that piece of non-information."† But, Jim Stoffels writes from Washington:

> A study of the full costs of missile defense conducted by two non-governmental organizations was just reported on January 3 at a Washington D.C. conference of the American Economic Association. The report finds that the likely cumulative cost of a "layered" missile defence system could be between $800 billion and $1.2 trillion.**

Stoffels was referring to a study that Richard F. Kaufman edited, *The Full Costs of Ballistic Missile Defense*, prepared for the Center for Arms Control and Non-Proliferation and the Economists Allied for Arms Reduction, with a preface by Kenneth J. Arrow, Nobel economics laureate of Stanford University.

What do you think? Should we believe David Pratt, or should we believe Nobel economist Kenneth Arrow and his fellow economists?

Further to the question of costs, the Center for Defense Information has reported that "the funding planned for developing and purchasing weapon systems from fiscal year 2003 through FY 2009 is more than $1 trillion, but the Missile Defense Agency portion is now spiraling beyond Congress' financial control . . . Congress has little ability to exercise its right of oversight and power of the purse. Missile defense truly has become a program beholden to no one and a law unto itself." This is because, thanks to Donald Rumsfeld, the "missile defense efforts have been exempted from Defense Department's normal rules for buying weapons systems."††

---

* February 17, 2004.

† *Hansard*, February 19, 2004.

** *Tri-City Herald*, January 24, 2003.

†† The CDI *Defense Monitor*, vol. XXXIII, no. 1.

On March 25, Reuters, as reported by Forbes.com, advised that a key component of the planned missile defence system

> has been beset by cost overruns and schedule slips for years. It could be considered a case study for how not to execute a space program.

Let's return to the question of American "electoral suicide." For those who anticipate Senator Kerry becoming U.S. president, there's good news and bad news. For the good news, although there's little that is specific at this writing, it appears that Kerry will at least temporarily reduce BMD funding and will probably delay some new construction (but would not cancel the program). He's also clearly on record as opposing "a new nuclear arms race [which would result from] building bunker buster bombs." Kerry also says he supports an international ban on placing weapons in space, and he supports steps to secure weapons of mass destruction, so they do not fall "into the hand of terrorists or hostile states." He says he opposes the Bush doctrine of pre-emptive war, and regards it as "a dangerous departure from the time-tested principles of American foreign policy."

Now come the doubters and the scary part.

According to University of Calgary political scientist Barry Cooper of the Centre for Military and Strategic Studies, even if John Kerry is elected president, U.S. policy in relation to "the establishment of ballistic missile defence . . . is not going to change next November, no matter who wins the White House."

According to John Isaacs, head of the Council for a Livable World, "Democrats have largely ducked" the issue of the Bush missile defence system. "That includes all of them that have been active in the past. Kerry was active." And he voted for missile defence in the Senate. According to the *Los Angeles Times*

> Democrats had planned to confront Bush on his plans to develop a missile defense program akin to Star Wars after he campaigned on

the issue in 2000. But they decided not to oppose the program after the Sept. 11 terrorist attacks.

Among Kerry's foreign policy positions is a promise to build up a greater U.S. presence in the South China Sea. (Remember the earlier warning about the dangers of U.S. policy towards Taiwan.) Beijing has always maintained that Taiwan is a part of China, yet the Taiwanese president says Taiwan is an independent and sovereign country where only 10 per cent of the population regards themselves as Chinese. While China now has 1,500 missiles aimed at the Island across the Taiwan Strait, George W. Bush has proclaimed that the United States would defend Taiwan in the event of an attack by China, and has been selling military equipment to the Taiwanese for years. The prospect of an American military buildup in the area can only be regarded as frightening. According to Robert McNamara, "There's absolutely no question in my mind that China will go to war with Taiwan if Taiwan appears to be moving towards independence. The U.S. would provide military assistance to Taiwan, and you would have a U.S.–China war."[*]

Now we come to Kerry and Canada. U.K. author and journalist John Laughland writes on March 8, 2004 (www.sandersresearch.com) that in a speech at UCLA on February 27, 2004, Kerry said

> If I am President, I will be prepared to use military force to protect our security, our people and our vital interests . . .

Laughland says "Kerry even seems to imply that military intervention might be conceivable in countries which are strong American allies.

> "We can't wipe out terrorist cells in places like Sweden, Canada, Spain, the Philippines or Italy *just* by dropping in Green Berets."

---

[*] Radio National, Washington, D.C., June 24, 2001.

Pardon. How's that again? What could he possibly mean? Do you think Paul Martin, Bill Graham, or Stephen Harper will ever ask him?

To be accused of being soft on defence is deadly in American politics and is considered by many Democrats as a kiss of death. Bill Hartung is a security and arms trade specialist at the New York-based World Policy Institute:

> I think missile defense is provocative, dangerous, and a waste of money; I think it should be relegated to the dustbin of history and we should get on with the business of nuclear disarmament. But unfortunately, that's a hard position to promote in official Washington because a lot of Members of Congress are still sort of stuck in the Cold War, and the Democrats in particular came to a position where they felt like they didn't want to be out-flanked by the Republicans; they don't want to be viewed as soft on defense.[*]

For a somewhat different perspective, here's Joseph Cirincione of the Carnegie Endowment for International Peace in Washington, D.C.:

> I think of missile defense as a con game, that this is basically a fraud, that they don't have something here, they don't own the bridge they're trying to sell you. They're selling you a promise, and it's a very appealing promise. I mean, who wouldn't want a defense against a ballistic missile if you could have one? I would like it. If there really was a system that would effectively intercept any ballistic missile aimed at me, or my country, I'd want to buy it. I'd also like a cure for cancer; I'd like a really good light beer, but some things are beyond our technological capability. I worked on the staff of the House Armed Services Committee for six years and then the Government Operations Committee for three years. I investigated and tracked ballistic missile defense programs for over nine years

---

[*] Ibid.

for Congress. I heard officials come up and swear that their program was ready to go. That it had been proved in concept, it had been technologically demonstrated, they just needed a little more money and a little more time. None of the dozens of systems proposed over those nine years ever worked. None of them. Ground-based lasers, free electron lasers, space-based lasers, chemical lasers, ground-based interceptors, space-based kinetic kill vehicles, these were all multi-billion dollar programs.

And from Theodore Postol, Professor of Science, Technology, and National Security Policy at MIT:

> This should be of profound concern to every U.S. citizen. The officers and program managers involved in developing the anti-missile system have taken oaths to defend the nation. Yet they have concealed from the American people and Congress the fact that a weapon system paid for by hard-earned tax dollars to defend our country cannot work.

And of profound concern to every Canadian should be the fact that our own government, our own military, and our own bureaucrats, knowing much of what you've just been reading, have been concealing the truth from the citizens of our country.

At least John Kerry appears to understand the underlying theme of what this book is all about:

> I mean either this is deadly serious or it is not. Now when you sit down with any expert, they'll tell you it's the most serious thing in the world. Well, if it is, why aren't we treating it as if it were? And we're not.[*]

---

[*] *New York Times*, May 30, 2004.

THE WRONG-HEADED PRIORITIES OF
GOVERNMENT ARE STUNNING AND INTOLERABLE

I want to know why there is always so much money for war and so little for the human condition.[*]

– Stephen Lewis

Okay, a bit more about dollars. As mentioned earlier, the U.S. by now has already spent up to $200 billion on ballistic missile defence and, with this massive amount of money, in the words of Ernie Regehr

> will have managed theoretical protection from a maximum of about 10-20 of the thousand-plus missiles and 7,000 warheads capable of hitting North America.

Let's consider all of this in the context of the Canadian provinces' urgent demands that Ottawa supply additional badly needed health care funding, the many months of waiting for MRIs, our doctor shortage, over-crowded emergency rooms and other well-documented serious health care issues, plus inadequate funding for social housing, for child care, post-secondary education, and other social problems.

[*] *Globe and Mail*, October 11, 2002.

After September 11, Ottawa introduced a $7.7 billion package of security measures. The 2003 budget promised an additional $1.7 billion for defence and the 2004 budget promised an additional $592 million for defence and security spending. Then, in April 2004, just before Paul Martin's visit to the White House, Ottawa announced another $690 million to beef up security. So, that's a total of just under a $10.7 billion increase in security and defence spending, while the provinces were desperately pleading for $2 billion to help them cover their health care shortfalls.*

Now, how much more would you like to spend on the American NMD program? And, where do you plan to get the money? Paul Martin said in his town hall meeting with Peter Mansbridge that "Ballistic missile defence is not going to cost Canada."

So, let's see now. We *must* be at the table so we can influence the American missile programs in a meaningful way, but we're *not* going to put up any money.† I suggest you quickly phone *Madly Off In All Directions*. Lorne Elliot will have a ball with that one.

Stephen Lewis said this:

> I want to know *why* there is always so much money for war and so little for the human condition.
>
> If we launch a war on Iraq, the world will find $7 billion, $8 billion, $10 billion, a month for bombing, but there's always a huge shortage of funds required to fight AIDS, malaria, tuberculosis.

Douglas Roche put it this way:

---

* As Graham Fraser reported in the *Toronto Star*, April 25, 2004, Joe Sokolosky of the Royal Military College has pointed out that Canada has spent a greater proportion on domestic security compared to the United States, yet got very little credit for it.

† "If we do participate, we can influence its development" said David Pratt in the House of Commons, February 19, 2004.

The wrong-headed priorities of government are stunning. They spend seventy times as much every year on preparing for and prosecuting war as on the entire United Nations system for peace.

And returning to the defence contractors and their political friends:

> The very idea that a small group of wealthy and powerful individuals should have the power over government policies that spend billions of dollars on military overkill while so many people live in life-threatening poverty is intolerable.

Last year, U.S. military spending was greater than the *combined* military spending of Russia, China, Japan, the United Kingdom, Saudi Arabia, France, Germany, Brazil, India, Italy, South Korea, Iran, Israel, Taiwan, and Canada, plus ten other countries. Since then, American military spending has increased by almost $50 billion, and plans are for at least a further $20 billion-a-year increase for the next five years.

As an aside, it's amusing to look back on Bush Senior and Dick Cheney's earlier comments about defence spending. President George H.W. Bush, in his January 1992 State of the Union address, said that his military expenditure cuts would mean that "By 1997 we will have cut defense by 30 per cent since I took office." Dick Cheney was Bush Senior's secretary of defense.

Fred Kaplan of *Slate* magazine writes that three days after Bush Senior's speech Cheney boasted of similar budget slashing:

> Overall, since I've been Secretary, we will have taken the five-year defense program down by well over $300 billion. That's the peace dividend . . . And now we're adding to that another $50 billion of so-called peace dividend.*

---

* *Slate* magazine, February 25, 2004.

Since Bush Junior was elected, the "peace dividend" has become the defence contractors' bountiful cornucopia instead.

In a press conference in New York on March 3, Stephen Lewis said that the World Health Organization urgently needs $200 million to put three million people into anti-retroviral HIV/AIDS treatment, but "Astonishingly, that support is not forthcoming."

> How is it possible that the resources for WHO can't be mobilized? 20 million people are already dead, 3 million people are begging for the right to cling to life. Another 3 million are behind them, and millions more after that, and we can't raise the one-tenth of 1 per cent of what we're spending on war and reconstruction in Iraq and Afghanistan, to break the back of a pandemic.
>
> If this project fails, as it surely will without the dollars, then there are no excuses left, no rationalizations to hide behind, no murky slanders to justify indifference. There will only be the mass graves of the betrayed.*

So, again, how do Canadians feel about defence spending and associated matters?

Most Canadians want good relations with the U.S. But, as indicated earlier, polls also show that their number-one foreign affairs priority is the protection of Canadian sovereignty. In the *Globe and Mail*'s words, Canadians "are particularly sensitive now to anything that smacks of buckling under to U.S. interests." This is of course why Paul Martin planned to delay the announcement about Canada's participation in the NMD program until after the federal election.

And, in an Ekos poll in October 2003, only 9 per cent of Canadians said that they would like Canada to be more like the U.S., 42 per cent said they would like Canada to be less like the U.S., and the rest said things should stay as they are now.

---

* *Toronto Star*, March 5, 2004.

So much for the Allan Gotliebs, the Tom d'Aquinos, the Wendy Dobsons, and the likes of Hugh Segal, Tom Courchene, Paul Tellier, Derek Burney, Brian Mulroney, Sherry Cooper, Gordon Nixon, Conrad Black, the Aspers, David Frum, Jack Granatstein, and John Manley, and so much for their "Big Ideas" and "Grand Bargains" and their other plans to integrate Canada even further into the United States. But, they all do have two important allies, Paul Martin, and Stephen Harper.

It's true, without question, George W. Bush has been a great friend, a great friend for Canadian nationalists. The Pollara Inc. poll in the February 9, 2004 *Maclean's* showed that given the opportunity, only 15 per cent of Canadians would definitely vote for him, while 40 per cent would definitely vote for someone else and 28 per cent would consider voting for someone else. Only 12 per cent of Canadians said Canada is better off with Bush as U.S. president, 43 per cent said we are worse off.

More recently, Paul Martin again repeated that the NMD system won't cost Canada anything. But the U.S. plans are *already* rapidly escalating an international arms race. To suggest that Canada's military spending won't have to be sharply increased as a result is either hopelessly naïve in the extreme, or intentionally misleading.

There is a suggestion that instead of putting up money when we join the American NMD plans, Canada will allow U.S. radar, missiles and other weaponry to be stationed on Canadian soil. Wonderful! We can save money in return for a surefire guarantee that our country will be a target in a nuclear war.

THE SWORD OF DAMOCLES:
DOESN'T CANADA HAVE TO CHOOSE
WHICH SIDE WE'RE ON?

Every man, woman and child lives under a nuclear sword of Damocles, hanging by the slenderest of threads, capable of being cut at any moment by accident or miscalculation or madness. The weapons of war must be abolished before they abolish us.
— John F. Kennedy to the U.N. General Assembly, 1961

Is there any reason why Canada must constantly be so timid, especially when so much is at stake, in voicing our opinions to Washington about foreign, defence, and military matters? American Ambassador Thomas Graham, Jr. is Senior Advisor at the Eisenhower Institute and former Special Representative of the U.S. President for Arms Control, Non-Proliferation, and Disarmament from 1994 to 1997, with a long, respected career in matters relating to the Nuclear Non-Proliferation Treaty, the ABM Treaty, and many other aspects of international arms control. Speaking in the summer of 2003 at the Couchiching conference, Ambassador Graham put it this way:

Many are now arguing for a space-based "boost-phase" defence system which would attack a missile shortly after launch . . . space to ground strike weapons, and thus a general arms race in space.

Canadians can help to avoid this.

> If *you* won't speak frankly to us, if *you* don't clearly and firmly tell us we're wrong ... *then who will?* Canada's unvarnished comments can help the United States to be the kind of world power that the world community hopes that it will be.

In a speech that I gave at the Woodrow Wilson Institute for Scholars in Washington,[*] I said to the American audience:

> You were wrong in Vietnam and your new pre-emptive first-strike policy is wrong today. You are wrong in ignoring or walking away from international agreements, wrong in your increasing unilateralism, wrong in your bottom-of-the-barrel foreign aid contributions.

Too bad Paul Martin will never say anything remotely similar. Too bad he will never say to the American president that the president's actions are *decreasing* security in the United States, in Canada, and in the rest of the world. Too bad that Martin won't urge Americans to discontinue their NMD and Star Wars madness, and ratify the Comprehensive Nuclear Test Ban Treaty and abandon their dangerous confrontational policy of pre-emptive attacks. And too bad Martin is afraid to tell Americans that the smartest thing they could do would be to completely, unequivocally disavow weapons in space. And too bad that Stephen Harper would never consider even thinking of any of it for even a single moment.

Today there are close to thirty thousand nuclear weapons in existence, with an informed estimate that the U.S. and Russia have over 96 per cent of them. We've gone through an extended period of making at least some modest progress in reducing nuclear arsenals and the likelihood that these horrendous weapons will actually be used. However, in March 2004 it was confirmed that

---

[*] November 2002.

The United States will not cut its nuclear arsenals to levels designated by the agreement concluded two years ago with Russia because "it must hedge against an uncertain future" according to a top administration official.

So now, instead of cutting back, we're rapidly heading in the opposite direction. On February 23, 2004, the *Seattle Post-Intelligencer* carried a truly frightening story by researcher and activist Glen Milner:

> The Bush administration favors a nuclear free-for-all, confident that it will be able to intimidate or destroy all adversaries with a varied arsenal of increasingly sophisticated weapons. Numerous international arms-control treaties, including the Anti-Ballistic Missile Treaty, the Comprehensive Test Ban Treaty and the Nuclear Non-Proliferation Treaty, have been abandoned or ignored by the United States.
>
> In November, Congress approved an administration request for continued research on nuclear earth-penetrators and a new generation of tactical nuclear weapons . . . By doing so, Congress and the administration repealed a 10-year-old ban on research for the development of new nuclear weapons . . .

One important result of the aggressive new American strategy will be the increased importance of the powerful Trident nuclear submarines

> A Trident missile can reach its target in 10-15 minutes, much faster than land-based missiles, aircraft or cruise missiles. . . .
>
> The secrecy of submarine deployment further advances the use of Trident missiles in a tactical strike. Those targeted likely would never know the missile was coming. . . .
>
> Nuclear weapons, even ones smaller than those used on Hiroshima or Nagasaki, will kill on impact and create a surrounding firestorm. The resulting radioactive dust will cause slow and agonizing death.

Do we Canadians *really* want to be part of this horrible mistake, this renewed threat if not guarantee of a nuclear catastrophe?

It's clear that most of the world is opposed to the American escalation of the arms race; doesn't Canada now have to choose which side it is on?

And, it is clear that the military-industrial complex that President Dwight D. Eisenhower warned about in 1961 is now firmly in control of the White House, the State Department, and the Pentagon as never before.* Do we Canadians really want to be part of their irresponsible, aggressive, and extraordinarily dangerous plans?

Does Canada need a military? Of course we do. But, as journalist Andrew Cohen wrote in his 2003 book, *While Canada Slept*:

> At the end of the day, we can have the world's best small military, its most generous, efficient aid program and its most imaginative foreign service. . . . We can equip ourselves to assume meaningful roles in mediation, peacekeeping, in reforming the United Nations, in alliances with like-minded Nordic countries and innovations to international financial institutions.

In *The Vanishing Country* I wrote

> We have to pay careful attention to what *our own* defence goals and priorities should be. Obviously we have to replace the ancient Sea King helicopters. . . . We need a permanent military presence in the Arctic. We need to beef up our long-range transportation capabilities.

But above all, wouldn't our very best defence strategy lie in helping less fortunate people around the world to the best of our ability?

---

* In a nationally televised address a few days before JFK's inauguration, Eisenhower warned about the dangers of the "unwarranted influence" of the close link between the U.S. military establishment and the arms industry.

Canada had a much-admired role as a middle power in the past; we should make our goal to reestablish ourselves as a middle power with no colonial baggage, no record of aggression, no long list of enemies, a country that promotes human rights and international agreements to promote disarmament and peace, helping the afflicted, and doing the best job we can to join with other countries to work towards the reduction of world poverty.*

Always we Canadians must keep one thing in mind. In defence policy, in foreign policy, and in trade policy, the multilateral forum route is *by far* the best strategy for our country. This is where Brian Mulroney led us so terribly astray with his comprehensive, multi-dimensional, straitjacketing Free Trade and NAFTA agreements. And this is one of the reasons why for the past fifteen years our role on the world stage has diminished dramatically, and why our current Liberal and Conservative political leaders think we somehow have to make up for Iraq by joining in the insanity of the new Star Wars plans. In May 2003, John Polanyi warned:

> The Canadian government, having held back from President George W. Bush's rush to war in Iraq, appears likely to join his rush to missile defence.

And it is quite evidently a rush since it's clear that the Americans are hurriedly deploying a very expensive weapons system without the smallest amount of evidence that there is any chance that it will work. John Polanyi continues:

> If Canada agrees to participate, it will be for political reasons. Having angered the Americans over Iraq, we must now placate them over missile defence. Neither Prime Minister Jean Chrétien nor his cabinet have troubled to convince Canadians of the NMD's

---

* *The Vanishing Country*, McClelland & Stewart Ltd., 2003, page 330.

worth . . . Liberal cabinet ministers have lined up to give laconic endorsements.

It is evident that NMD points the world down the wrong path . . . Unchecked, weapons and counterweapons lead only to the development of further weapons . . .

The international control of armament offers the only protection for the weak, as for the mighty.

But dare we tell the emperor that he has no clothes? It would be an act of friendship were we to do so.*

Polanyi was prescient. I spoke to two Liberal cabinet ministers who asked not to be identified. Both said the arguments against the NMD were convincing, but ultimately the decision would be "political," meaning that Paul Martin's desire to cozy up to the U.S. would be the decisive factor.

So, all things considered, what *should* Canada's role in the world be? First of all, we should quickly back away from any involvement in the American NMD plans. Moreover, we should join with many like-minded nations in opposing Bush's plans on the grounds that they will lead to rapidly escalating insecurity and growing nuclear confrontation. With the NMD, the world will become a much more dangerous place, with a much greater potential for horrendous nuclear carnage.

We Canadians should help organize a major international conference in Vancouver, to strongly condemn the weaponizing of space. We should invite Russia, China, India, Brazil, the Scandinavian countries, and many others to join us in a massive worldwide campaign against U.S. plans.†

We should tell Washington that Canada intends to lead a new campaign for disarmament and for the destruction of all nuclear

---

* globeandmail.com, May 7, 2003.

† I suggest Vancouver because a large number of excellent people, with the encouragement of the City Council, are already planning a World Peace Forum for 2006, and a proposal for a widely endorsed Space Preservation Treaty. The conference would be organized much as the 1997 Land Mines Treaty Conference in Ottawa.

weapons, reminding them of the 2000 Review Conference on the Non-Proliferation Treaty, which promised an "unequivocal undertaking to accomplish the total elimination of nuclear weapons." We should tell the Americans that they made a terrible mistake walking away from the ABM Treaty and that we plan to invite the U.S. and Russian presidents to an early summit meeting in Ottawa in an attempt to have the treaty reinstated.

And we should tell everyone that Canada intends to greatly increase our humanitarian foreign aid, make a strong commitment to future participation in a permanent United Nations peacekeeping force, and that in the future we will be much more forceful in the UN in opposing the slaughter of innocent men, women, and children in both military aggression and via terrorism.

We should also make it clear that we Canadians will step up our dedication to the multilateral Conference on Disarmament, to the 188-nation Nuclear Non-Proliferation Treaty, and to the Comprehensive Test Ban Treaty, and that we will include in our plans for the Vancouver conference proposals to organize an international treaty to ban all missile tests, and to criminalize all sales of components needed to create nuclear weapons. As Ernie Regehr has written:

> The threatened proliferation of weapons of mass destruction and intercontinental range ballistic missiles should lead Canada to re-emphasize that its security is inextricably linked to a stable, rules-based international order that needs to function, not according to the whims of the powerful, but in the service of the common good.
>
> Canada needs to return to and rely upon the nuclear disarmament fundamentals that it has so long articulated; to pursue as a diplomatic priority the delegitimation of nuclear weapons and [pursue] continued, irreversible reductions in strategic arsenals.

Arms control and disarmament agreements must become an international priority. In the January/February 2004 *Literary Review of Canada*, Lloyd Axworthy wrote that Canada should be a convenor of international humanitarian intervention efforts, organizers of global efforts to establish new laws and standards, a reformer at the UN, an idea maker putting forward solutions to serious issues such as disarmament and global climate change and the rights of children, and a builder of networks to tackle specific issues of global importance.

Canada can help build an effective international justice system making the international economic system more democratic and fair.

The 2000 Pugwash Group and Science for Peace seminar made clear in a letter to Jean Chrétien what Canada's role should be.

Canada should continue to push the nuclear weapons states, particularly its nuclear neighbour . . . on measures to achieve total nuclear disarmament. To show its own deep commitment, Canada should publicly refuse to participate in all nuclear systems preparations. It should unequivocally announce that it will not participate in the envisaged ballistic national missile defence system. This will be a breath of much needed fresh air in nuclear proliferation discussions.

Canada should continue to foster the human security approach and a worldwide culture of peace that should totally replace the current outmoded dependence on weapons of mass destruction and mass murder.[*]

In March 2004, Dr. Paul Hamel and Dr. John Valleau of Science for Peace wrote

The U.S. military has invaded 31 countries since the end of WWII. It is now the plan to wield this projection of unilateral power from space, where lethal weapons are to be positioned as part of the misnamed missile defence system. In Canada CEOs continue to agitate

---

[*] March 22, 2000.

for further Canadian integration into this aggressive U.S. military-industrial system. What becomes of Canada's heartfelt commitment to ban weapons from space, to abolish nuclear weapons and land mines, and to resolve conflicts peacefully through the UN, if we are instead to be integrated into the military and economic apparatus of a nation demonstrably opposed to these principles?

Canada has been a leader in the opposition to weapons in space for over thirty years. Just as we led the way in the Anti-personnel Landmines Treaty, we should now lead the way to a strong international commitment by all nations to oppose the weaponization of space. We are in an ideal position to do so. James George, Dr. Carol Rosin, and Alfred Webre write:

> As seen from space, Canada lies between Russia and the United States, and, geography aside, no country is in a better position to initiate international action. Since 1982, Canada has led the growing United Nations lobby opposing weapons in space.
>
> With the strong support of UN Secretary-General Kofi Annan, the UN General Assembly last Nov. 29 voted 156-0 to prevent an arms race in space.
>
> On Sept. 28, 2001, Russian Foreign Minister Igor Ivanov had invited "the world community to start working out a comprehensive agreement on the non-deployment of weapons in outer space." At the UN Conference on Disarmament in June last year, China had taken a similar position.
>
> But neither Russia nor China will initiate binding action while the United States is unbound. If Canada does not act now, who will? If we do, we will generate far more support and respect than we gathered over our land mines initiative. We could turn the tide that will lift all ships and preserve space as a weapons-free commons.[*]

---

[*] *Toronto Star*, April 30, 2002. The three authors represent the Institute for Cooperation in Space. See www.peaceinspace.com

In a nutshell, Canada's place should indeed be at the table, the dis-armament table, rather than becoming part of a dangerous new arms race.

Thirty thousand children die *each day* of easily preventable illness. Five hundred thousand women die, mostly unnecessarily, in pregnancy or childbirth every year. Thirteen million children were killed by diarrhea in the 1990s, more than all the people lost in armed conflict since the end of the Second World War. Three million men, women, and children died of AIDS last year, and 1.7 million died of tuberculosis. Over one million children died of malaria.

There are twenty-five countries where more than 15 per cent of all children die before they reach the age of five. There are twenty-three countries where more than 30 per cent of all children below the age of five are underweight. There are eleven million children orphaned by AIDS in sub-Saharan Africa; most are unable to attend school. There are thirty-three countries where over 50 per cent of the population does not have adequate sanitary facilities. In the world's forty-two highly indebted countries, per capita income is less than $1,500 a year.[*]

Imagine how very many lives could be saved if developed countries only met their long-standing, commonly-agreed-to goal of 0.7 per cent of GDP for foreign aid. The U.S. contribution alone would increase by a massive $60 billion. Instead, the U.S. contributes only one-tenth of 1 per cent of GDP to aid.

In an excellent article in the February/March 2004 *Mother Earth News*, Lester R. Brown points out that by shifting less than 8 per cent of global military spending, we could properly fund

> Universal primary education in the 88 developing countries that require help, the basic shortfalls in health care costs, family plan-ning, reproductive health, adult literacy, AIDS prevention education and condom distribution, school lunch programs for the 44 poorest

---

[*] *The State of the World's Children*, UNICEF, 2004.

countries, and assistance for preschool children and pregnant women
in these countries.*

That's less than 8 per cent of military spending!

According to World Bank President James Wolfensohn, world
defence spending amounts to around $900 billion a year, while total
foreign aid is only about $60 billion. "That seems to me to be the most
nonsensical thing you can imagine."†

Canada has little to be proud of in its recent record. Our foreign
aid contribution has dropped from 0.53 per cent of GDP in 1975 all the
way down to 0.28 per cent in 2002. One thing all Canadians should do
is ask Paul Martin, with all his repeated pious rhetoric about world
poverty, how is it that when he became finance minister in 1993,
Canada stood in fifth place in terms of our foreign aid contributions
and now, directly as a result of his actions in the Department of
Finance, we're down to thirteenth place, and we've also fallen down the
list to thirty-eighth place among ninety-four nations taking part in
UN-led peacekeeping missions?**

Tonight, some 840 million men, women, and children will go to bed
with empty stomachs. Think of that in terms of the terrible hunger and
suffering of the equivalent of twenty-seven times Canada's entire population. It's hard to imagine. And think of the fact that at the same time
there's a global surplus of food.

Is there a surefire way for we Canadians to build a surefire defence
to make us safer, including safer from terrorism? There is, and it has
nothing to do with the aggressive militarism of George W. Bush, Donald
Rumsfeld, and the Pentagon, and it certainly has nothing to do with the
NMD schemes. We should make a much greater effort to feed starving
children and to contribute to their health care. We should work hard to

---

* www.motherearthnews.com

† Yahoo News, April 27, 2004.

** Jonathan Gatehouse, *Maclean's*, May 3, 2004.

decrease the obscenely generous Western world's agricultural subsidies and reduce our barriers to imports from poor developing countries. We should go to work with like-minded countries (and there are many of them) to strengthen international institutions and agreements, and work hard towards the badly needed and long overdue reform of organizations such as the WTO, the World Bank, and the International Monetary Fund.

Canada was the first country with the technological capacity to create a nuclear bomb to renounce that opportunity. From the very beginning our country strongly opposed the creation of nuclear weapons. How things have changed! As recently as March of 2000, then Canadian Ambassador for Disarmament Christopher Westdal gave a speech in Vancouver about Canada's role in disarmament:

> We want the coming conference of the Nuclear Non-Proliferation Treaty to promote and protect the treaty universality. . . . Canada will make commitments to build conviction and political will in support of nuclear disarmament and non-proliferation.

How unlikely it now seems that Paul Martin or Bill Graham or David Pratt's successor will ever take meaningful actions to achieve these goals. Instead, they appear rapidly headed in blinkers in the opposite direction. Terrence Edward Paupp (in www.WagingPeace.org) writes

> With the deployment of NMD an international reaction will most likely result in a new arms race. With the continuation of these trends, the tragic consequences of the Cold War, which ended in 1990, will only worsen with a second Cold War at the dawn of the 21st century. If continued spending on weapons increases and expands under NMD, there will be a corresponding depletion of human capital, as social programs and investments in health, education, and welfare, are cut even deeper. This, in turn, will result in the inevitable widening of circles of poverty and a growing gap

between the haves and the have-nots. Such an outcome will probably produce revolts, revolutions, and rising levels of terrorism
around the globe.

It seems to me that the choice for Canada is clear. Do we continue our
decades-long policies of working for peace, for disarmament, and for
binding multilateral agreements to de-escalate the dangers of nuclear
war, or do we hitch our destiny to aggressive American unilateralism, to
their policy of abandoning multilateral treaties and dismissing arms
control and developing even more weapons of mass destruction and
turning space into a violent military and nuclear frontier?

Moving by Stealth to Co-operate in Our Own Ghastly Annihilation

———————■———————

The unleashed power of the atom has changed everything save our modes of thinking and we thus drift toward unparalleled catastrophe.

— Albert Einstein

If you do not take action to make the world the place you want, it really doesn't matter what you feel.

— Betty Williams, Nobel Peace Prize laureate

Sixty years ago, Nobel laureate Niels Bohr, who worked on the Manhattan Project, said

The terrible prospect of a future competition between nations about a weapon of such formidable character can only be avoided through a universal agreement.*

———————

* The Manhattan Project was the Second World War project to develop the first nuclear weapons. The design and construction of the bombs took place at Los Alamos, New Mexico. The first bomb, untested, was dropped on Hiroshima on August 6, 1945, the second on Nagasaki three days later.

President John F. Kennedy, in a speech to the United Nations General
Assembly in 1961, said

> We must create worldwide law and law enforcement as we outlaw
> worldwide war and weapons. . . . For peace is not solely a matter of
> military or technical problems – it is primarily a problem of politics
> and people. And unless man can match his strides in weaponry and
> technology with equal strides in social and political development,
> our great strength, like that of the dinosaur, will become incapable
> of proper control – and like the dinosaur, vanish from the earth. As
> we extend the rule of law on earth, so must we also extend it to
> man's new domain – outer space. . . . The new horizons of outer
> space must not be driven by the old bitter concepts of imperialism
> and sovereign claims. The cold reaches of the universe must not
> become the new arena of an even colder war.

How remarkably different from the words, philosophy, and actions of
George W. Bush and his aggressive colleagues in the White House and
Pentagon! Today, Mohamed ElBaradei says the only solution is "multi-
national controls" on all materials used to create nuclear arms. William
J. Broad, writing in the *New York Times* about the actions of the nefari-
ous Pakistani scientist Dr. Abdul Quadeer Khan says

> Never before has the nuclear black market been found to operate
> with such startling impunity and thoroughness. This time it offered
> complete kits – raw uranium, machines for enriching it, and even
> blueprints for how to turn nuclear fuel into atom bombs.[*]

The United Nations Secretary-General Kofi Annan recently warned
that "the possibility of nuclear war is a very real and very terrifying
possibility." The Canberra Commission on the Elimination of Nuclear
Weapons said

---

[*] February 15, 2004.

The risk of use of nuclear weapons has increased, and the proposition that nuclear weapons can be retained in perpetuity and never used – accidentally or by decision – denies credibility.

I began this book with a quote from the Mayor of Hiroshima. Tadatoshi Akiba went on to say

Given U.S. intransigence, other nuclear weapon-states appear to be reevaluating the need for such weapons.

Therefore, it is incumbent upon the rest of the world, the vast majority of the international community, to stand up now and tell all of our military leaders that we refuse to be threatened or protected by nuclear weapons. We refuse to live in a world of continually recycled fear and hatred. We refuse to see each other as enemies. We refuse to co-operate in our own annihilation.

We demand here and now that . . . regardless of any nations that may oppose it, there be a call for the de-alerting of all nuclear weapons, for unequivocal action towards dismantling and destroying all nuclear weapons with a clearly stipulated timetable, and for negotiations on a universal Nuclear Weapons Convention establishing a verifiable and irreversible regime for the complete elimination of nuclear weapons.

In a move no doubt intended to deflect the mounting criticism, Bill Graham announced just prior to the February 2004 House of Commons vote calling for Canada to suspend NMD talks with the U.S., that he has written to the other Group of Eight countries asking them to join Canada in a move at the UN Conference on Disarmament in Geneva to keep space free of weapons.

Cynical? Graham knows full well that the United States will *never* agree to such a proposal. Hypocritical? It is most unlikely that Graham has ever made such a demand directly to his friend Colin Powell, or to other senior officials in Washington. Repeated phone calls to the minister's office enquiring about the U.S. response to his proposal have produced many promises to provide the requested information, but eventually only a vague, noncommittal reply was received.

Once Canada joins in the NMD program, and when Graham or his successor is forced to admit that the U.S. is not the slightest bit interested in such a proposal, no doubt they will simply continue the nonsensical fiction that NMD has nothing to do with weapons in space.

Only a few years ago, back in 1998, 117 world leaders, including Mikhail Gorbachev and Jimmy Carter, agreed to work toward the complete abolition of nuclear weapons. Canada, rather than joining the Bush/Rumsfeld NMD program, should denounce the dangerous American plans. Canada should combine with the many other nations that would readily and enthusiastically agree, to build a strong new international coalition to abolish all weapons of mass destruction, beginning first with all missile systems for their delivery and a systematic program of taking all nuclear weapons off alert and placing them into storage with international inspectors allowed to verify and regularly monitor what is happening. Then, the ultimate step must be the destruction of all such weapons.

How to make such a proposal happen? Only strong trade, investment and other economic sanctions could ever make it work. Only the firm resolution of scores of nations can make it a reality. Of course the skeptics will say it can never be done. Most people with children and grandchildren will say it *must* be done. (If you're not yet convinced, be sure to read Appendix Three.)

In March of 2000, in a series of speeches across Canada, Christopher Westdal eloquently warned of the terrible dangers of nuclear weapons facing the world:

> I want to invoke the continuing clear and present danger of nuclear arsenals, and the unrelenting threat they pose to my life and yours.
>   We need to stop believing that nuclear deterrence provides any enduring solution to the singular, ghastly security problem we have

now faced for a lifetime, and been very lucky to survive. We have to stop believing we can go on being lucky indefinitely . . . with the human future held fickle hostage to our luck.

The more nuclear weapons there are, and the further they spread, the greater the unutterable risk over time that they will fall into hands evil enough to use them.

We don't seem to like to think or talk much about all of this, but the hard fact is that devastation unto human extinction could be unleashed through the use – in accident, fear or anger – of any major part of our immense nuclear arsenal.

On May 24, 2002, Presidents Bush and Putin signed the Strategic Offensive Reductions Treaty (The Moscow Treaty), which, despite the title and the ample ballyhoo, did not require any reduction of nuclear forces – not a single device, warhead, silo, submarine, bomb or bomber. Moreover, although some reduction in the operational status of nuclear weapons was promised, remarkably there was no verification process built into the treaty!

According to the Council for a Livable World, one of the U.S.'s pre-eminent arms-control organizations focusing on halting the spread of weapons of mass destruction,

Like it or not, nuclear deterrence is likely to be with us during the first part of this century, as it was during much of the last. But, the United States may more often be the deterred rather than the deterrer should it seek to involve itself militarily in regions where there may be others with nuclear capabilities and interests opposed to it. We think it important that Americans recognize that the United States may not hold all the high cards and that it will have to face the reality that the costs of getting its way on all points of difference with adversaries may be higher than its citizenry are willing to pay. Beyond deterrence, its choices in dealing with North Korea as an emerging nuclear power will be by negotiation or pre-emptively destroying North Korea's offending capabilities, with all the risks of massive civilian casualties and political costs that that would entail.

It is illusionary to see an ABM defense system as an escape from this dilemma.*

Have things changed in relation to the principle of deterrence, the long-standing idea that if you have enough destructive weaponry of your own, you will discourage any prospective attacker (MAD, mutually assured destruction). Christopher Westdal addressed this point during his cross-Canada speaking tour in March 2000:

> As recalled in *Canada and the Nuclear Challenge*, the December 1998 Report of the Standing Committee on Foreign Affairs and International Trade, nuclear deterrence might be quite stable, all things relative, in a studied bilateral standoff, two players, a chess game like the Cold War's. But in our emerging new world, with more nuclear players, the game becomes more like cards, poker, say, far less predictable, with luck a larger factor. And should the struggle against proliferation be lost, should there ever be many players, well then it'd be like roulette with nukes, with luck over time a decisive factor.
>
> Another problem with nuclear deterrence is that it is a disgrace. Nuclear arsenals *may* have been necessary; they have always been evil – and unconscionably dangerous. The sin in them is indiscriminate killing: murder. Nuclear arsenals are a deep stain on the human legacy. It is true – as is regularly, passively observed – they cannot be uninvented. Neither, for that matter, can poison or high buildings – but that doesn't mean we need keep a lethal cupful at every lip or crowd to the edge of high roofs – all the better to jump.

---

* clw@clw.org, February, 2004.

For Tariq Rauf

there are mounting concerns in Canada about becoming "locked-in" to an unforeseen future involving U.S. NMD, with unknown costs that would be difficult for Canada to disengage from.

For Canada, the decision will be a "defining moment."

A key concern is to ensure that the debate is a well-informed one. This requirement itself is problematic.*

Problematic? How can there *possibly* be an informed public when the government is either telling citizens very little, or providing misleading information about the nature of NMD and its clear implications for weapons in space, a renewed arms race, and nuclear proliferation?

In December 2003, the Liu Institute at the University of British Columbia issued a press release signed by Lloyd Axworthy and Ernie Regehr.

A new report by an international team of strategic and defence experts says Canada is "moving by stealth" to support the American government's controversial Ballistic Missile Defense initiative.

The experts panel, which includes John Polanyi, former Canadian Ambassador for Disarmament, Peggy Mason, and Victoria Sampson of the U.S. Center for Defense Information, is alarmed by Canada's decision to abstain from a recent United Nations resolution expressing concern that missile defences could negatively impact nuclear disarmament and non-proliferation efforts and lead to a new arms race in outer space.

"The decision to abstain is an ominous indication of the direction in which the government is headed on BMD" says Lloyd Axworthy.

---

* *Canada's Perspective on NMD*, forum on the Missile Threat and Plans for Ballistic Missile Defense, Rome, Italy, January 2001.

And where are Stephen Harper and the Conservative Party on all of this? The Conservatives are rushing madly off in the same direction as the Martin government, but they want to get there quicker. Here's Jay Hill, MP for Prince George-Peace River, the party's national defence critic, during the February 17, 2004 House of Commons debate:

> I find myself in complete agreement with everything the Minister of Foreign Affairs has stated in his remarks tonight. The only question I have for the minister is, what took you so long? I would suggest that they have had eight years to discuss this issue . . . it is incumbent upon the government to get on with things.
>
> I believe the missile defence program is the most peaceful option available to counter the threat of ballistic missile attacks.
>
> We have been on the record for quite some time now saying that we should be involved in this.

Now, here's Hill's colleague MP Stockwell Day, (Okanagan-Coquihalla) the Conservative's "shadow minister of foreign affairs" from the same Commons debate:

> To say that we should not be involved in these discussions makes no sense, no common sense, no strategic sense, and no foreign policy sense. . . . A ballistic missile defence system mutually assures protection . . . it would be naïve beyond description to abandon our responsibilities to provide for the safety and security of our citizens by staying outside the system. . . . We need to be there. It would be delinquent for us not to be.

And, understand this:

> Why would belligerent nations spend money to develop ballistic missile capabilities when they would know they would face an array of defence systems that would easily knock them down.

Stockwell Day is not exactly renowned for his depth of knowledge on how "easily" ballistic missiles could be knocked down. Returning to the question of Liberal "stealth," here's Jay Hill again in the House of Commons on February 17.

> I find it troubling that a government department appears to be pushing full steam ahead on the same project for which the Prime Minister and his government claim to be weighing the options, and seeking further public input. These claims do not seem credible if at the same time a federal department has been given the go-ahead to proceed on missile defence.

By stealth? We learn from Beijing that

> In the dying days of his government, former prime minister Jean Chrétien quietly authorized a move that surprised and baffled some of his top diplomats: He joined a U.S.-led scheme of dubious legality that could trigger military confrontations with North Korean ships on the high seas.
>
> Although virtually unnoticed by the public, the plan has provoked deep divisions in Canada's foreign-policy establishment, provoking fears that it could pave the way for a U.S.-led military blockade of North Korea, with the potential of dragging Canada into a war.
>
> Insiders said the government failed to consult its diplomats or heed their concern when Ottawa bowed to U.S. pressure to join the scheme to intercept North Korean ships on the high seas.[*]

Then we learn that Canada is spending $700,000 to help Raytheon develop new radar, that we are planning to place a multi-million dollar satellite in orbit which would become part of the U.S. Space Command's

---

[*] *Globe and Mail*, February 16, 2004.

surveillance network, and that our Department of National Defence is suggesting we develop our own space "kill vehicles" to ensure Canadian firms share in the American NMD contracts. Earlier, in a complete reversal of previously stated policy,

> Canada is talking to Washington about the use of Canadian soil for stationing interceptor rocket launchers and radar stations as part of a continental ballistic missile defence program . . . in lieu of a major cash contribution if the Federal government decides to join the program.*
>
> Until now, federal officials have said that Canadian participation would not involve Canadian territory or a cash contribution.†

And, what if Stephen Harper and the Conservatives had won the June 28 federal election? Not only would they have moved Canada towards full military and foreign policy integration with the U.S., but Harper, who boasts that he is "a gung-ho, ideological, pro-American"** and has lamented the fact that Canada didn't send troops to join in the Iraq war ("a serious mistake"), would quickly take major steps to integrate Canada even further with the U.S. economy. This would likely include an extensive array of Canadian policies, regulations, and standards harmonized to those in the U.S., a customs union, energy and resource integration, and steps towards a two-tiered health-care system (Harper's right-hand man, Tom Flanagan, believes that Canada should scrap medicare). Also, in a country that is already one of the most decentralized federal nations in the world, Harper would hand over even more power to the provinces, weakening the national government to a point where its ability to act in the national interest is severely constrained, and he would almost certainly drastically

---

* Possible sites are reported to be Goose Bay, Iqaluit, Alert, or somewhere else on Ellesmere Island.

† *Globe and Mail*, February 23, 2004.

** See Lawrence Martin, *Globe and Mail*, June 3, 2004.

weaken legislation relating to foreign ownership, foreign control, and Canadian culture.

For Harper "The United States . . . is the world leader when it comes to freedom and democracy."*

In concluding a talk in October 2002, Christopher Westdal said

Nuclear weapons did not go away with the Cold War. They are with us still, in their grotesque hair-triggered thousands, enough for the blasphemy of human and much other extinction on this exquisite planet – and as they spread, the ghastly precedent of their use looms.

Nuclear arms control is faltering. Vitally important trends have soured. And nuclear disarmament, essential to our safety now and to our survival long-term, is a literally vital, but currently receding goal. Make no mistake: for you and your children and theirs, this is very far from good news.

I don't think we can go on this way. I think it is unconscionably and unnecessarily dangerous – and well beneath the dignity required for human survival.

You should know that your government is working hard to confront, counter and roll back these threats to our security. We are much heartened in our work to know that Canadians have faced these facts unblinking and that we carry on with their informed hope, their political support, and their heartfelt backing.

Christopher Westdal has been so forceful and articulate for so many years on the dangers of nuclear weapons that he deserves much praise. But, alas, as far as political support for nuclear disarmament is concerned, everything has changed. Paul Martin and his government, though they will strenuously deny it, are apparently prepared to abandon Canada's decades-long commitment to controlling arms and supporting multilateral agreements. And in doing so, as I have spelled out, they are

---

Globe and Mail, May 29, 2002.

not being forthright with Canadians. Back to Douglas Mattern: earlier this year, in an article in *War & Peace Digest*,* Mattern wrote

> Terrorism of the 9/11-type tragedy is a serious and dangerous problem that people understand, and they take caution when the color alerts are issued. What's amazing is that the same people ignore a far greater terrorism that is on Red Alert every day with millions of lives and a billion tears but an hour away.
>
> This is the terrorism posed by nuclear weapons.
>
> This warning takes on a new urgency due to the expansion of the nuclear weapons club, and most ominous, the "pre-emptive" war policy of the Bush administration that includes the possible use of nuclear weapons. Military analyst William Arkin writes that the Bush administration's war planning "moves nuclear weapons out of their long-established special category and lumps them in with all the other military options."
>
> The Bush team is also determined to build a new generation of tactical nuclear weapons. The U.S. has already resumed production of plutonium pits for nuclear bombs for the first time in 14 years, and the Bush team has plans to resume nuclear testing at the Nevada underground site.
>
> Our compliant, corporate-serving, and pusillanimous Congress has allocated the funds for this escalation in the massive 2004 military budget.
>
> In today's Red Alert world more than 30,000 nuclear weapons are stockpiled, including thousands of U.S. and Russian nuclear warheads that are on a "hair-trigger" alert, ready to be launched in a few minutes notice, that would destroy both countries, and much of civilization, within an hour.
>
> Is this the kind of civilization we want or that can endure with any promise for future generations? Surely an observer from another world would conclude the ancient Greeks were right: "Whom the

---

* *War & Peace Digest*, February 1, 2004.

gods would destroy, they first make mad." Perhaps the years of this terror are too difficult to comprehend and leaves people immune to the danger, a mental numbness, if not passive "madness."

The miserable failure to end the nuclear madness and the criminal waste of our wealth and resources on militarism has caught up with us. Time is running out, and the reckless escalation and "preemptive" policy by the Bush administration makes it imperative that people mobilize and collectively demand immediate action before it is forever too late!

But instead, the American military are now pushing for the resumption of nuclear weapons testing. A U.S. resumption of tests almost certainly means the end of the Comprehensive Test-Ban Treaty and would result in a massive, long-term wave of Russian, Chinese, Pakistani, and Indian tests. Without question, states that are now non-nuclear will embark on nuclear weapons tests. An epidemic of proliferation will surely result.

Will there *really* be a national debate in Canada about Bush's NMD plans, or did our government, as many suspect, make its mind up long ago, but was waiting until after the federal election to tell Canadians that we are joining in Bush's scheme? As indicated earlier, according to Paul Martin

> There will certainly be a debate, a national debate before any final agreement is signed. We want to be at the table so we know what's going on because it's only if we have that, that you can have a valid national debate. Canadians are entitled to be consulted and there will be that debate.*

In a December 18, 2003 letter to a friend in Edmonton, a senior representative of the Prime Minister promises that the Martin government will focus on

---

* CBC Television, February 6, 2004.

ensuring Canada's independent role in the world as one of pride
and influence in order to advance our values and promote Canada's
independent voice abroad.

That would be excellent. But, in the Liberal caucus of Jean Chrétien,
John Manley was referred to as "Governor Manley" because of his
strong, pro-U.S. policies. But before he withdrew from the leadership
race, Manley accused Paul Martin of "pandering to the U.S. . . . he plans
to sacrifice too much to please the U.S." This, incredibly, from a man
who wants Canada to deepen its ties with the U.S., commit to joining
the BMD system, enter into a customs union with the U.S., harmonize
Canadian and U.S. health care (!) and safety regulations and standards,
remove restrictions on legal, financial, and communications services. In
other words, give up completely on the idea of Canada.

In *The Vanishing Country* I spelled out in some detail that when
Paul Martin became prime minister, he would move Canada much
further towards integration with the U.S. in economic policy, in energy,
in foreign and military policy, in a whole host of areas, standards, and
policy harmonization.

In the *Globe and Mail*, February 24, 2004, we read "PM looks at
closer relations with the U.S.: Blueprint calls for policy co-ordination."
So what Brian Mulroney began with the historic Free Trade Agreement,
and what Jean Chrétien enthusiastically endorsed with NAFTA, Paul
Martin will even more quickly move towards, with much further and
much deeper integration with the United States. And Stephen Harper
will be pushing him from behind.

In the face of all the abundant evidence why Canada should not join
the American NMD system, Paul Martin wants to climb aboard because
it is fully consistent with his long-standing attitudes towards much
closer Canadian-American relations and greater harmonization of the
two countries' policies and values.

In the Senate on March 9, 2004, Douglas Roche emphasized how
critically important Canada's decision with respect to the United States
BMD plans will be.

First, participation in BMD will constitute Canadian endorsement for the weaponization of space. The U.S. Missile Defense Agency charged with developing missile defence, is perfectly clear on this point. BMD will be an integrated system. The system is to involve a layered defence, capable of intercepting missiles in boost phase shortly after launch, in mid-course in space, and in terminal phase as they near the target. As a recent study by the American Physical Society pointed out, a land-based missile defence system will be incapable of intercepting missiles in boost phase launched from distant states. To account for this deficiency, the U.S. will have to deploy weapons in space.

It should come as no surprise, then, that the Missile Defense Agency has requested funding for research in 2005 aimed at developing space-based weapons, with the stated intention of deploying a test bed in space . . . The deployment of such a test facility will smash the long cherished and widely held norm against weapons in space.

With the inevitable resulting buildup of nuclear arms, there will certainly be a very substantial increase in current arsenals.

This has led the noted American defence analyst, Dr. Bruce Blair, of the Center for Defence Information in Washington, to declare ". . . every BMD interceptor missile in the ground will be another nail in the coffin of nuclear disarmament."

Moreover,

. . . If we cannot extract an American guarantee not to weaponize space before agreeing to participate, how will we be able to obtain such a guarantee afterwards?

especially when David Pratt's letter to Donald Rumsfeld "with the objective of including Canada as a participant in the current U.S. missile defence program" promised that Canada's participation

... will not remain limited to the system being deployed in 2004, but "will evolve over time, and our bilateral co-operation in this area should also evolve."

On March 18, 2004, an open letter to Paul Martin signed by a long list of well-known Canadians said

> We, the undersigned, are deeply alarmed that our government continues to pursue Canadian involvement in the development of the U.S. missile defence system.
>
> Canadian involvement in U.S. missile defence would undermine decades of Canadian efforts to rid the world of nuclear weapons. As such, it would directly collide with the wishes of the Canadian people who have expressed overwhelming support for nuclear disarmament.
>
> It would require the reversal of a 30-year Canadian policy opposing the weaponization of space. The Bush administration's plans for missile defence expressly include the placement of space-based weaponry. The most recent U.S. budget specifies an intent to develop a space-based missile "test bed," beginning as early as 2005.
>
> While we understand the government's desire to improve Canada–U.S. relations, we firmly believe that the political and economic benefits of Canadian integration in missile defence would be far outweighed by the long-term negative consequences for global security, and for Canadian sovereignty over future foreign affairs and defence matters.
>
> By devoting vast resources to developing a missile shield, the United States is ignoring the real causes of insecurity, and is likely to aggravate existing grievances. Security for us all would be much better served by rejuvenating multilateral efforts to stop the spread of nuclear weapons and uphold international law, and by addressing the root causes of conflict and terrorism such as civil strife, global inequality, and environmental degradation.

As a good neighbour, Canada should be working to convince the U.S. that true and lasting security cannot be achieved through military might. No missile shield could ever ensure the safety of North America.

True security can only be achieved by establishing relationships of mutual respect and co-operation, free of exploitation, with nations and peoples throughout the world.

That is what we as Canadians, have always believed and proudly stood for. And that is the kind of Canada that we want now and in the future. Mr. Martin, we implore you – and all Canadians – to keep Canada out of missile defence.

On April 29, 2004, the *Globe and Mail* reported that just prior to Paul Martin's White House meeting with President Bush, the Canadian government made it clear to Washington that Canada would sign on to the U.S. NMD plans, but the Liberals wanted this kept secret until after the election, since it's "a vote loser" according to an unnamed adviser.

When the announcement is finally made it will be disguised as simply an extension of existing NORAD co-operation. The claim will somehow also be made that Canada's participation will allow it important influence and involvement in the decision-making process with respect to the launching of missiles. According to the *Globe*, sources have suggested that Canada's participation in the missile defence program itself "is essentially a foregone conclusion, and that the only real issue now is timing."

The *Globe* also reported that one recent study from the Department of Foreign Affairs and the Defence Department suggested that the U.S. missile defence system would lead to the deployment of weapons in space. And in July we learned that a February report commissioned by Foreign Affairs warned that the U.S. missile defence plans would unquestionably lead to a new worldwide arms race.

While treated as front page news, none of this was new. Most of those following comments from Bill Graham, David Pratt, and the Prime Minister in the House of Commons or in the defence committees already understood that despite all of the mounting evidence, the Martin government had long-before made up its mind. The repeated claims that the government hadn't yet made a decision and that more consultations and studies were necessary to allow it to do so, were simply more misleading Liberal obfuscation.

In 1997, Jody Williams won the Nobel Peace Prize for her work in the banning and destruction of anti-personnel mines. In a spring 2003 article, she wrote:

> Asked to opine about what I think is one or two of the biggest issues facing us in the coming decades might be, I find myself needing to quote Arundhati Roy, in her anti-nuclear polemic *The End of Imagination*. Roy writes, "There's nothing new or original left to be said about nuclear weapons. There can be nothing more humiliating for a writer of fiction to have to do than restate a case that has, over the years, already been made by other people . . . and made passionately, eloquently and knowledgeably." She goes on to say, however, that she is "prepared to grovel. To humiliate myself abjectly, because in the circumstances, silence would be indefensible."

Jody Williams continues:

> I also find myself willing to try on some issues – on which I am not even approaching what could be called "an expert." The one that causes me particular concern is the open embrace by the Bush administration of national missile defense (NMD) . . . the Son of Star Wars. The cold-blooded horror of militarizing space.
>
> As Betty Williams, Nobel Peace Prize laureate and founder of the Northern Ireland Peace Movement has said, emotions without action are irrelevant. If you do not take action to make the world the place you want, it really doesn't matter what you feel.[*]

---

[*] *Los Angeles Times* Syndicate International, June 20, 2001.

Albert Einstein said "The world is dangerous not because of those who do harm, but because of those who look at it without doing anything."

Now, not later, now is the time for Canadians to take a firm stand to ensure the survival of the country that we love as a proud, independent, sovereign country.

An essential place to begin is to say NO to the National Missile Defense plans, and to say YES to a proud and sovereign Canada.

And now is the time for all Canadians to go to work, as hard and as effectively as we possibly can, to make sure that our world is not enveloped in a catastrophic nuclear apocalypse.

Let's not let the madmen take control of our destiny and destroy our future, the future of our children and our grandchildren, and the future of our world.

Appendix One

Brief History and Current Status of the American Star Wars Program

———◼———

Paul Hellyer, former defence minister, writes

> It is almost 40 years since U.S. secretary of defense Robert McNamara asked me if Canada would be interested in helping develop an anti-ballistic missile defence for North America. I was able to say "Thanks, but no thanks," which was the position of the Pearson government."*

More recently, formal missile defence plans began over twenty years ago with Ronald Reagan's "Strategic Defense Initiative" which promised to create a "perfect shield" to protect the U.S. from Russian intercontinental ballistic missiles. As previously indicated, the government of Brian Mulroney also turned down invitations to become involved in U.S. plans. It was soon evident that, despite the huge and rapidly increasing expenditures, there were no reasonable expectations that the Reagan system would ever be effective. The project was abandoned soon after the fall of the Soviet Union.

President Bill Clinton, in the election year 1996, proposed a new missile defence program including three years of research to be followed

---

* www.canadiandimension.mb.ca, May 15, 2003.

by three years of construction. The Clinton program spent many more billions, but accomplished little, including zero in the way of techno-logical breakthroughs to allow any confidence that an effective missile defence was something that could be achieved. In May of 2000 a team of eleven American scientists completed a year-long study of the pro-posed system with the warning that what was happening in Washington was "a real scandal" because it had long been very obvious that the pro-posed system wouldn't work:

> The reality is that any country that is capable of building a long-range missile and has the motivation to launch it against the United States would also have the capability and motivation to build effective countermeasures to the planned defense. To assume other-wise is to base defense planning on wishful thinking.[*]

I am indebted to the Center for Arms Control and Non-Proliferation, and the Council for a Livable World, both in Washington, D.C., for the following March 10, 2004 update, titled *Status of Missile Defense Program.*

Current national missile defense deployment plans
The initial deployment of land-based interceptors designed to smash into enemy warheads headed towards the U.S. is scheduled for calendar 2004. The Pentagon originally announced plans to deploy 10 interceptors in Alaska and California by October 2004, just before the election. At this point, it is likely that the Administra-tion will deploy fewer than 10 interceptors by that date, but declare the system operational earlier in the year when a few interceptors are in place (*Washington Post*, Feb. 2, 2004). Six of the interceptors are slated for Fort Greely in Alaska and four at Vandenberg Air Force Base in California. Up to 30 more interceptors are slated to be deployed in 2005 and 2006 at these two sites and a third unnamed site. The present plan calls for one Aegis cruiser to be

---

[*] Physicist David Wright and Theodore Postol of MIT, *Boston Globe*, May 11, 2000.

operational by 2005 with five SM-3 missiles for theater or short-range missile defense.

Administration's latest budget request
The request for fiscal 2005 is $10.2 billion, the largest single Pentagon weapons program and a 13% increase over the fiscal 2004 program. About $3.2 billion of that would go to the ground-based mid-course system (GMD) that is slated to be deployed later this year. If the Space Based Infra-Red System-High (SBIRS-high) is included, the total request for missile defense for the next year is $10.7 billion.

Potential attacks to be defended
The initial deployment is designed to protect against an attack from one or two nuclear warheads launched from North Korea.

Testing of national missile defense
The system to be deployed later this year has undergone eight intercept tests (trying to hit a target in space). All these tests have occurred in a highly scripted, unrealistic test environment. The tests included simple targets, only a few decoys and used an unrealistic target missile trajectory. Moreover, because of the pressure to deploy this year, four of the six intercept tests originally planned to be held by October 2004 have been canceled since deployment was announced in December 2002. In all, the Missile Defense Agency has eliminated nine of 20 planned intercept tests, citing a shortage of missiles and other factors.

Technical difficulties with deployment in 2004
The system has not even completed its development tests, much less its operational tests under real world conditions.
The booster rocket for the system has suffered many development problems, and is behind schedule.

A ground-based X-band radar needed to enhance satellite tracking is not scheduled to be fielded until 2005 at the earliest.

An infrared satellite system capable of tracking incoming missiles and helping guide the interceptor will not be in place for many years. The system cannot deal with decoys and countermeasures.*

What the Pentagon's testing office says

Thomas Christie, director of the Pentagon's Office of Operational Test and Evaluation, produced a skeptical view of the system to be deployed. From a January 21 Bloomberg article by Anthony Capaccio, "The U.S. missile defense system may not work when it's deployed Oct. 1, the Pentagon's top weapons tester says. Tests to date haven't really challenged the ground-based system, and two intercepts slated this year leave 'very limited time' to show key components are capable, Thomas Christie says. 'Even with successful intercepts in both these attempts, the small number of tests would limit confidence' in the interceptor missiles and their hit-to-kill warheads to perform as part of an integrated system, Christie writes in his annual assessment of major U.S. weapons programs . . . 'Delays in production and testing of the two boosters design have put tremendous pressure on the test schedule immediately prior to fielding,' Christie writes. 'At this point, it is not clear what mission capability will be demonstrated prior to initial defensive operations.'"

What the General Accounting Office says

According to a *New York Times* article of September 24, 2003: "The Bush administration's push to deploy a $22 billion missile defense system by this time next year could lead to unforeseen cost increases and technical failures that will have to be fixed before it

---

* As well, production delays make it likely that the full schedule for missile delivery will not be met.

can hope to stop enemy warheads, Congressional investigators said yesterday. The General Accounting office, in a 40-page report, said the Pentagon was combining 10 crucial technologies into a missile defense system without knowing if they can handle the task, often described as trying to hit a bullet with a bullet. The report especially criticized plans to adapt an early warning radar system in Alaska to the more demanding job of tracking enemy missiles, saying it had not been adequately tested for that role. The overall uncertainty, the investigators said, has produced "a greater likelihood that critical technologies will not work as intended in planned flight tests."

Is deploying something better than nothing?

Defense Secretary Donald Rumsfeld has argued that an incoming missile defense is better than none at all: "I think that it is certainly better to have that capacity than to not have it." (December 17, 2002 press conference). Premature deployment may well give both policy makers and the American people a false sense of security. If a military confrontation with a nuclear-armed adversary broke out in a few years, it is not hard to imagine that American leaders will rely on a missile shield as French leaders mistakenly relied on an inadequate Maginot Line before World War II.

The most recent plans at this writing call for the deployment of a very limited system of six silo-based anti-missile interceptors at Fort Greely near Fairbanks, Alaska and four at the Vandenberg Air Force Base in California by the end of 2004, the total number expanding to twenty in 2005.

As well, early warning radars are deployed at the RAF Station in Fylingdales in England and Thule in Greenland. (A more detailed historical review can be found in the chapter "Shield of Dreams.")

Fred Kaplan, writing in *Slate* magazine, underlines what we already know:

In the past six years of flight tests, here is what the Pentagon's missile-defense agency has demonstrated. A missile can hit another missile in mid-air as long as (a) the operators know exactly where the target missile has come from and where it's going; (b) the target missile is flying at a slower-than-normal speed; (c) it's transmitting a special beam that exaggerates its radar signature, thus making it easier to track; (d) only one missile has been launched; and (e) the "attack" happens in daylight.

Beyond that, the program's managers know nothing – in part because they have never run a test that goes beyond this heavily scripted (it would not be too strong to call it "rigged") scenario.

Kaplan might have added (f) so long as there aren't a number of decoys and (g) so long as multiple independently-targeted warheads aren't employed, and (h) so long as radar-jamming devices aren't used, and etc. and etc and etc.

Let's contrast this with the kind of bunk DFAIT is issuing as in this press release of January 4, 2004:

Five of eight tests of long-range interceptors have succeeded.

A few days later, from the U.S. Missile Defense Agency:

There has been another successful test flight (from Kwajalein Atoll, Republic of Marshall Islands, in the central Pacific).
[But] no intercept took place.

Some "success!"

In early 2004, Canadian physicists warned Paul Martin that the American NMD has little chance of working and could very well prove to be a danger to Canadians. The 1600-member Canadian Association of Physicists wrote to Paul Martin with their conclusion that the NMD wouldn't be effective, citing their newly completed four-hundred-page study. The letter also pointed to the possibility of partially disabled missiles crashing and exploding in Canada.* Earlier, both the American Physical Society representing U.S. physicists, and the entire editorial staff of *Scientific American* magazine produced highly critical studies of the Pentagon's plans.

* *Toronto Star*, April 4, 2004.

APPENDIX TWO

VALUABLE INTERNET SITES WITH RESPECT TO THE WEAPONIZATION OF SPACE, NUCLEAR WEAPONS, U.S. MILITARY PLANS, ETC.

———■———

Readers who would like to be added to my regular monthly updating e-mail list should contact me at mhurtig@telusplanet.net. I usually send out three or four items a month.

The sixteen-page United States Space Command's "Vision for 2020," with dramatic illustrations in full colour, has been withdrawn from the Space Command's Web site. But, you can still get it at www.gsinstitute.org, go to Documents, then to Vision 2020.pdf. I suggest you send it on to Paul Martin, to Bill Graham, and to Stephen Harper and ask them for their response. You can reach Graham at Graham.B@parl.gc.ca, Martin at Martin.P@parl.gc.ca, and Harper at Harper.S@parl.gc.ca. You might want to include Hill.J@parl.gc.ca, and Day.S@parl.gc.ca.

Readers who may wish further details with respect to U.S. Department of Defense and Air Force plans for space should go to the Federation of American Scientists site at http://www.fas.org/spp/ military/dsb.pdf for the eighty-two-page *Report of the Defense Science Board/Air Force Scientific Advisory Board Joint Task Force on Acquisition of National Security Space Programs* (May 2003) from the Office of the Under Secretary of Defense for Acquisitions, Technology and Logistics. The report was approved and forwarded to Donald Rumsfeld. The document opens with the note that

Recent operations have once again illustrated the degree to which U.S. national security depends on space capabilities. We believe this dependence will continue to grow. . . . We see no viable alternative to the unique capabilities that space systems provide.

For further reading go to http://www.rand.org/publications/MR/ MR1209/ where you will find *Space Weapons Earth Wars* by five authors on the Rand Corporation's Web site. Also worth noting is the U.S. Missile Defense Agency at www.winbmdo.com and the Arms Control Association at www.armscontrol.org.

For a seventy-four-page report on how the U.S. is planning a new generation of nuclear weapons, go to www.clw.org and click on New Nuclear Weapons.

For the most complete official U.S. document on the NMD scheme and the weaponizing of space, the 176-page November 2003 U.S. Air Force report, described by Leonard David, may be found by going to the Washington, D.C., Center for Defense Information, www.cdi.org, and clicking on the document describing the detailed U.S. Air Force "Transformation Flight Plan." Or go to www.af.mil.

All these documents make for very scary reading. All are deadly serious and quite clear about their intentions.

For readers who want to continue to follow developments related to the topics in this book, I mention again that the Center for Defense Information (CDI) in Washington, D.C., is invaluable. Their Web site at www.cdi.org is updated frequently. On this site you will find a four-page, first-class description of the *U.S. Air Force Transformation Flight Plan*, which is the best concise analysis of American plans to weaponize space. For some of the more obtuse people at DFAIT and the Department of National Defence, CDI has produced *Space Weapon Related Programs in the U.S. 2005 Budget Request*. Another site worth bookmarking is the *Bulletin of the Atomic Scientists* at www.thebulletin.org.

In March 2004 the Center for Defense Information produced a long, detailed, and chilling document by Jeffrey Lewis, Executive Director of the Association of Professional Schools of International Affairs. The study, titled *What if Space Were Weaponized? Possible Consequences for Crisis Scenarios*, shows how "the use of space weapons could lead to a rapid escalation of hostilities – possibly even to nuclear war." The document which reminds readers that

> Beijing and Moscow have pressed for negotiations in the Conference on Disarmament in Geneva on the issue of "preventing an arms race in outer space." The U.S. position has been that there is no space arms race currently underway and that negotiations are unnecessary.

Returning briefly to DFAIT (www.dfait-maeci.gc.ca) and to another of their absurd press releases, we learn that while

> Russia initially voiced serious concerns over U.S. plans for BMD . . . Russia has been discussing BMD co-operation with the United States . . . *

Theresa Hitchens of the CDI, writes

> Under the administration of President George W. Bush, there has been increasing emphasis by U.S. government officials of the perceived need for the United States to prepare for eventual war in space. U.S. Space Command and Missile Defense Agency plans already envision the deployment of space-based weapons as integral parts of future U.S. arsenals.
>
> Even the U.S. Air Force's own space war games up to now have concluded that potential negative consequences from the use of space weapons – including the possibility of triggering a nuclear response from an enemy – cannot be dismissed.

The CDI document's Executive Summary makes two salient points.

---

* January 15, 2004.

The Pentagon is moving forward with a number of research efforts to develop the capabilities to fight a war in, through, and from space, and yet there has been almost no public discussion of the costs vs. benefits of such a strategy.

And,

In a world with space weapons, the United States may be better armed, but we may well be less secure.

It is important to understand [that] . . . if the United States pursues these capabilities, other nations almost assuredly would too.

Contrast these words with DFAIT's constant refrain that in their attitude towards NMD:

The Government is committed to ensuring and enhancing the security of Canada and Canadians.

Paul Hellyer puts it well:

The notion that NMD will save Canadian lives is unquestionably the most far-fetched of all the arguments.*

Another site worth looking at is www.space4peace.org, the site for the Global Network Against Weapons and Nuclear Power in Space. Books, videos, information packages, and updates are available. Another good site is the Institute for Cooperation in Space at www.peaceinspace.com. Also excellent is the Center for International Policy at www.ciponline.org. Certainly among the most consistently valuable sites are The Council for a Livable World at www.clw.org, the Carnegie Institute at www.ceip.org, and the Union of Concerned Scientists at www.ucsusa.org. This site has a list of Space Weapons Resources on the Web.

---

* Speech, May 15, 2002.

Canadian sites you should monitor are www.ploughshares.ca, www.ceasefire.ca, http://scienceforpeace.sa.utoronto.ca/, www.ligi.ubc.ca, www.pugwashgroup.ca, www.middlepowers.org, and www.stopwar.ca.

You might also want to visit Waging Peace.org and two quite opposite sites, the American Ballistic Missile Defense Organization at www.acq.osd.mil/bmdo/ and the U.S. Strategic Command at www.statcom.af.mil/.

Jim Stoffels's site is www.wcpeace.org.

And by all means don't forget to regularly monitor www.viveleCanada.ca, our Web site devoted to Canadian sovereignty, which, though relatively new, is already getting 195,000 hits a month.

APPENDIX THREE

"ROGUE STATES," TERRORISTS, AN ACCIDENT WAITING TO HAPPEN, AND WHY DESTROYING ALL NUCLEAR WEAPONS *MUST BE* THE ONLY ANSWER.

───────■───────

It's widely known that the public excuse for building the National Missile Defense system is the danger of an attack on the U.S. by a "rogue state." The president of the Center for Defense Information, Dr. Bruce G. Blair, in an article titled "Rogue States: Nuclear Red-Herrings," addresses the subject:*

> For all the talk about rogue states acquiring nuclear weapons to threaten the United States, and all the heated debate about the United States developing mini-nukes and bunker busters to keep rogues at bay, the U.S. nuclear weapons establishment does not pay much attention to the "axis of evil." The real obsession of the U.S. nuclear enterprise at all levels – from Strategic Command in Omaha to the bomb custodians and designers in New Mexico – is keeping U.S. nuclear forces prepared to fight a large-scale nuclear war at a moment's notice with . . . Russia.
>
> The dirty little secret of America's current nuclear policy is that 99 per cent of the nuclear weapons budget, planning, targeting, and operational activities still revolves around this one anachronistic

---

* Center for Defense Information, *The Defense Monitor*, vol. XXXIII, no. 1.

scenario. The rationale is a throwback to the Cold War, but however absurd, it still is the axis of current nuclear operations.

Scratch Russia from the list of enemies – as it should be – and all justification for maintaining a large U.S. nuclear arsenal evaporates.

There would be no planning to build a new factory possibly in New Mexico – to produce plutonium triggers by the hundreds annually to support a U.S. arsenal of thousands of nuclear bombs. The drumbeat to resume nuclear testing to ensure the reliability of aging bombs would end. The drive to develop new bunker busters, reputedly to target rogue states but really meant to put at risk high-level nuclear command bunkers inside two mountains in Russia, would lose its impetus. The many tens of billions of dollars spent each year on operating and upgrading the thousands of U.S. bombs would be saved.

The United States and Russia currently possess 96 per cent of the world's total inventory of 30,000 nuclear weapons. Most of the remainder belongs to U.S. allies and friends – Britain, France and Israel. The combined arsenals of Pakistan and India, with whom the United States enjoys reasonable relations, represent a small fraction of 1 per cent. That leaves China, hardly an enemy, whose 1 per cent of the world's total includes 20 long-range missiles that could hit the United States (compared to 6,000-plus U.S. nuclear weapons that could reach China today). Then there is North Korea, which possibly has a couple of weapons but no missiles or planes capable of dropping them on U.S. targets. The other prolif-erant states of concern – notably Iran – do not yet possess a single nuclear bomb.

A small fraction of the current U.S. arsenal of 10,650 bombs would amply cover all plausible nuclear threats to the American homeland, U.S. allies and interests overseas, if only the idea of fighting a large-scale nuclear war with Russia received the ridicule it deserves. Reasonable people not only scoff at the obsolete idea that the United States must be prepared for such a war in order to deter it, but also appreciate the many unnecessary risks incurred by clinging to this outdated world view.

This anachronistic nuclear thinking has perpetuated the risky practice of keeping a hair-trigger on early warning and decision-making, as well as nuclear missile forces. Warning crews in Cheyenne Mountain, Colo., are allowed only three minutes to judge whether initial attack indications from satellite and ground sensors are valid or false. Judgments of this sort are rendered daily, as a result of events as diverse as missiles being tested, or fired – for example, Russia's firing of Scud missiles into Chechnya – peaceful satellites being lofted into space, or wildfires and solar reflections off oceans and clouds. If an incoming missile strike is anticipated, the president and his top nuclear advisors would quickly convene an emergency telephone conference to hear urgent briefing. For example, the war room commander in Omaha would brief the president on his retaliatory options and their consequences, a briefing that is limited to 30 seconds. All of the large-scale responses compromising that briefing are designed for destroying Russian targets by the thousands, and the president would have only a few minutes to pick one if he wished to ensure its effective implementation. The order would then be sent immediately to the underground and undersea launch crews, whose own mindless firing drill would last only a few minutes. These tight timelines for decision-making at all levels are driven by only one scenario – a sudden, massive Russian attack.

The risks of launching on false warnings, or by some unautho-rized action, posed by this pressure-packed, decision-making-by-checklist may have been acceptable during the Cold War, but not today. Why carry such high risks if they stem from a totally ficti-tious threat? Ironically, the U.S. hair-trigger posture forces Russia into an identical stance, and the risks of a false alarm on the Russian side have grown since the end of the Cold War due to the steady deterioration of its early warning and command system. By acting as though Russia may intentionally attack, the United States is exposing itself to a real threat of unintentional Russian attack.

By keeping thousands of nuclear weapons fueled, armed, targeted, and ready to fire upon receiving a couple of short computer signals, the United States and Russia are further playing roulette with another real danger: nuclear terrorism. Keeping weapons cocked on hair-triggers raises many terrifying questions in the light of the global terrorist threat. Could terrorists spoof U.S. or Russian early warning systems, causing false alarms and semi-automatic responses that lead to and over the brink of nuclear war? If scores of heavily armed Chechens could take over the theater in Moscow, could terrorists seize mobile intercontinental Russian missiles, figure how to circumvent the safeguards, and fire them? Could terrorists electronically hack into missile launch circuits from remote locations, or into the communications network used to command strategic missiles, and cause an unauthorized launch?

If these scenarios sound far-fetched, remember that foresight of terrorist scenarios is much less than perfect, as the Sept. 11, 2001 hijacking revealed. And consider this: A past Pentagon review found a gaping hole in the computer security of a Navy radio network used to transmit launch orders to U.S. nuclear missile submarines. The investigation found that unauthorized persons, including terrorist hackers, might be able to slip electronically inside the network, seize control over the radio transmitters, and illicitly send fake orders to the boats. The deficiency was deemed so serious that the sub launch crews had to be given elaborate new instructions for validating launch orders, in order to ensure that they would not fire upon receipt of phony orders.

All of the thousands of U.S. and Russian launch-ready weapons only represent an accident waiting to happen and a temptation to terrorists to gain control over them. Maintaining these large, cocked arsenals is not needed to prevent a nuclear war between the United States and Russia, nor does it deter terrorists or provide a useful tool in fighting them. Doing so instead represents a grave danger to the civilized world if these weapons fall into the wrong hands.

Russia is no longer the enemy. We deny this truth at our own peril and expense. Facing and accepting this truth lights a path to deep nuclear reductions and true security.

As Dr. Blair indicates, nuclear proliferation brings with it the terrible and growing dangers of an accident. Frequently we've read about poor nuclear weapons security in Russia. Here's another perspective from the Center for Defense Information:

Accidents happen, including accidents with U.S., nuclear weapons. In some cases, the warheads were lost – the United States lost at least two nuclear weapons during aircraft crashes in 1958 off the coast of Savannah, Georgia, and in 1966 off the coast of Spain. In other cases, warheads have been recovered: In 1996, an Energy Department tractor trailer overturned in a blizzard in Nebraska carrying "classified cargo" – later confirmed to be several nuclear warheads. Fortunately, the weapons were recovered undamaged after several hours. These kinds of accidents are more likely to happen when forces are kept on alert and moved around.

Doug Mattern writes about another terrifying scenario, this time reflected in an actual event.

This month marks the 20th anniversary of an incident that could have resulted in nuclear war. The forgotten hero that singularly avoided this disaster through his cool judgment under incredible pressure is Lt. Colonel Stanislav Petrov, formerly of the Soviet Army.

It was the night of September 26, 1983, with Colonel Petrov in charge of 200 men operating a Russian early warning bunker just south of Moscow. Petrov's job was monitoring incoming signals from satellites. He reported directly to the Russian early warning-system headquarters that reported to the Soviet leader on the possibility of launching a retaliatory attack.

It's important to note that this was a period of high tension between the U.S. and the Soviet Union. President Reagan was calling the Soviets the "Evil Empire." The Russian military shot down a Korean passenger jet just three weeks prior to this incident, and the U.S. and NATO were organizing a military exercise that centered on using tactical nuclear weapons in Europe. Soviet leaders were worried the west was planning a nuclear attack.

In an interview with the English newspaper *Daily Mail*, Colonel Petrov recalls that fateful night when alarms went off and the early warning computer screens were showing a nuclear attack launched by the United States. "I felt as if I'd been punched in my nervous system. There was a huge map of the States with a U.S. base lit up, showing that the missiles had been launched."

For several minutes Petrov held a phone in one hand and an intercom in the other as alarms continued blaring, red lights blinking, and the computers reporting that U.S. missiles were on their way. In the midst of this horrific chaos and terror, the prospect of the end of civilization itself, Petrov made an historic decision not to alert higher authorities, believing in his gut and hoping with all that is sacred, that contrary to what all the sophisticated equipment was reporting, this alarm was an error.

"I didn't want to make a mistake," Petrov said "I made a decision and that was it." The *Daily Mail* wrote, "Had Petrov cracked and triggered a response, Soviet missiles would have rained down on U.S. cities. In turn, that would have brought a devastating response from the Pentagon."

As agonizing minutes passed, Petrov's decision proved correct. It was a computer error that signaled a U.S. attack. In the *Daily Mail* interview, Petrov said, "After it was over, I drank half a liter of vodka as if it was only a glass, and slept for 28 hours," and he commented,

"In principle, a nuclear war could have broken out. The whole world could have been destroyed."

In our increasingly superficial societies that praise celebrities and all manner of fools as role models, many legitimate heroes go unnoticed and without reward. In the case of Colonel Petrov, he was dismissed from the Army on a pension that in succeeding years would prove nearly worthless. Petrov's superiors were reprimanded for the computer error, and in the Soviet system, all in the group were automatically subjected to the same treatment.

The *Daily Mail* found Petrov's health destroyed by the terrible stress of the incident. His wife died of cancer and he lives alone in a second-floor flat in the dreary town of Fyranzino about 30 miles from Moscow.

"Once I would have liked to have been given some credit for what I did," said Petrov, "but it is too long ago and today everything is emotionally burned out inside me. I still have a bitter feeling inside my soul as I remember the way I was treated."

There have been many incidents like September 26, 1983; just how many we may never know. We do know that little has changed as thousands of U.S. and Russian nuclear warheads remain on "hair-trigger" alert that could be launched in a few minutes' notice destroying both countries in less than one hour – perhaps initiated by a computer error.

To end this utter madness all nuclear warheads must be moved from "hair-trigger" alert and placed in storage with continuous inspection by both sides and the United Nations. Only then will the daily threat of nuclear incineration by an accidental missile launch or miscalculation be eliminated.

In an interview with Stanislav Petrov on *Dateline* NBC (Nov. 12, 2000) reporter Dennis Murphy said: "I know you don't regard yourself as a hero, Colonel, but, belatedly, on behalf of the people in Washington, New York, Philadelphia, Chicago, thank you for being on duty that night."